Healing Wisdom from the Afterlife

"*Healing Wisdom from the Afterlife* is a banquet for the soul! Sharing vulnerable testimony, spiritual insights, moving stories, and compassionate guidance, Alexandra Leclere bravely leads readers into the spiritual world that constantly surrounds us but is usually ignored. Read this book, and you will discover passages that speak directly to your life. I enthusiastically recommend *Healing Wisdom from the Afterlife* for anyone seeking solace and wisdom."

JULIE FAITH PARKER, PH.D., AUTHOR OF *EVE ISN'T EVIL*
AND EDITOR OF *MY SO-CALLED BIBLICAL LIFE*

"Alexandra Leclere's *Healing Wisdom from the Afterlife* is a wise, lovely, and deeply informative addition to the outpouring of modern literature now raising the curtain on the grand stage of the Greater Reality. Rooted in Leclere's personal and professional experiences, written in accessible language, and amplified by the wisdom acquired through ancient and modern practices, this book helps us decode the workings of our incarnations and discover how best to navigate the 'pinball machine' of life on Earth."

DANIEL DRASIN, AUTHOR OF
A NEW SCIENCE OF THE AFTERLIFE

"In her latest book, *Healing Wisdom from the Afterlife*, Alexandra Leclere impressively presents how to maneuver through life using communication with the spirit world. Using poignant examples drawn from her extensive client list and her personal experiences, she shows how we can make sense of our personal lives, both the good and bad aspects. I encourage everyone to read this book and learn how to understand the journey that life has presented. You may just learn to enjoy the journey you are on."

CLAY DINGER, CONSULTING HYPNOTIST AND
AUTHOR OF DO YOU KNOW YOUR SELF(S)?

"*Healing Wisdom from the Afterlife* is an empowering and actionable guide to accessing spiritual wisdom within your own life. Through intimate anecdotes, Alexandra shares her insights and illuminates the mechanisms of the path and purpose of spirits. The depth of knowledge it imparts is truly transformative. I highly recommend this thoughtful and enlightening book."

TANIA DAVIS, VISUAL ARTIST

Healing Wisdom

from the

Afterlife

How to Communicate
with the Spirit World

ALEXANDRA LECLERE

Destiny Books
Rochester, Vermont

Destiny Books
One Park Street
Rochester, Vermont 05767
www.DestinyBooks.com

Destiny Books is a division of Inner Traditions International

Copyright © 2024 by Alexandra Leclere

All rights reserved. No part of this book may be reproduced or utilized in
any form or by any means, electronic or mechanical, including photocopying,
recording, or any information storage and retrieval system, without permission in
writing from the publisher.

Cataloging-in-Publication Data for this title is available from the Library of Congress

ISBN 978-1-64411-890-0 (print)
ISBN 978-1-64411-891-7 (ebook)

Printed and bound in the United States by Lake Book Manufacturing, LLC

10 9 8 7 6 5 4 3 2 1

Text design and layout by Priscilla Harris Baker
This book was typeset in Garamond Premier Pro with Gill Sans, Gotham,
Heirloom Artcraft, and Legacy Sans used as display typefaces

To send correspondence to the author of this book, mail a first-class letter to the
author c/o Inner Traditions • Bear & Company, One Park Street, Rochester, VT
05767, and we will forward the communication, or contact the author directly at
alexandraleclere.com.

Scan the QR code and save 25% at InnerTraditions.com.
Browse over 2,000 titles on spirituality, the occult, ancient
mysteries, new science, holistic health, and natural medicine.

To my mom who taught me faith; my grandchildren Sammy, Jayce, Katia, Alexa, Ben, and Maddox, who hold our future; and to my children, Tania, Tristan, Terence, and Talia, who are my everything.

And, of course, Georges Leclere.

Contents

INTRODUCTION

A Game of Pinball

IT WAS DARK AND I KNEW I WAS FALLING, as the car I was in somersaulted through the air and hit the ground with a resounding crash, just to fly off again like an Olympic gymnast flipping over and over and over again. Each time, it hit the ground harder. The car seemed to be endlessly falling, as I was tossed around inside it like a ball in a pinball machine. Every time we struck the ground my body slammed into a different part of the car's interior. Then a car window shattered in front of my face. My mind was spinning as I tried to understand what was happening. Finally there was one more huge crash and then everything went quiet.

> *I love Paris in the summer when it sizzles.*
> *I love Paris every moment,*
> *Every moment of the year.*
>
> COLE PORTER

I was twenty-two and had been doing graduate work in Paris at the Sorbonne. It was fabulous! I loved everything about it. There is certainly nothing better than to be young and single in Paris. One of my classmates, Wassim, and I became study friends. Wassim was from the Middle East, a part of the world that was a mystery to me. He needed a master's degree to further his career. I had come to Paris to get my master's degree too. We were united in our determination to succeed.

One day Wassim offered to read my palm. Laughing, I allowed him to review its secrets. I didn't really believe that he actually had that talent, but it was a good time to take a study break. I was hopeful that he would say some encouraging things to me. To my great surprise he spoke to me about an accident that I'd survived when I could have died. Besides not being pleased to hear this, I had no memory of any such accident. He said it had taken place when I was about twelve. "No!" I insisted. Nothing like that had ever happened to me. Of course I would remember something that traumatic. He told me to think about it. And then perhaps to change the subject, he started to tell me about who I would marry. I wasn't really sure I wanted to hear any more from him, but I braced myself and listened.

Wassim declared that I would marry someone who was very well known and had very important international connections. This was music to my ears. I was young and interested in marriage at some point in my life, and the man he described sounded interesting. At least he didn't say I would never find anyone, and I'd be really sad about it. Saying goodbye to Wassim that day I felt happy thinking about the man I would someday marry.

It took a week for the horrible memories of the car accident to come into my consciousness. My father had been driving my mother and me back to Ohio after our summer vacation in Florida. My brothers had escaped this vacation because they had football practice. They were overjoyed to miss the arduous trip, sweating in the hot car as our parents argued. Being twelve, I had no choice in the matter.

I don't remember anything about the trip down. It was the usual drive, and Florida had been the broiler oven it always was in August, except that year Dad invested in suntan lotion and even an umbrella. Despite these precautions he got burned to a crisp as usual, and so did I.

Mom liked to stop at every roadside attraction and scenic turnout, and there were lots of them between Ohio and Florida. We had already stopped at a number of these turnouts on the way home, and we were in Kentucky, driving through some mountainous terrain when we saw a sign for another scenic turnout with an exceptional view.

Mom insisted that we stop. Dad said no. Mom kept insisting. Finally she pulled me into the argument by telling Dad that I wanted to take a photo of the view. I wasn't really interested in taking a photo, but I understood that I had to agree with Mom if I knew what was good for me. I don't think I actually said anything, but Mom carried on, declaring that I had a new camera and I needed to take a photo.

Angrily my father went to the scenic turnout. As we drove to see this supposedly spectacular mountain view, I remember sitting in the back seat horrified at the awful fight that had just taken place between my parents. Dad stopped the car, and my mother yelled at me to hurry up and take the photo as though all this had been my idea to begin with. Dutifully I jumped out of the car and took a photo. It was the last one on my roll. I got back into the car. As I was rewinding the film into its protective cylinder Dad angrily pressed the pedal to the floor. The car jerked and swerved as Dad tried to regain control of it. I remember the crunching sound of the tires and my father frantically turning the steering wheel as we drove off the edge of the cliff where I had just taken the photo.

As the car summersaulted through the air, I remember tumbling around in the back of the car thinking, *This is really bad!* A window smashed in front of my face, then there was complete silence.

My mother called out my name. "Are you okay?" she asked.

"Yes," I answered.

She called to my father. He didn't answer. She called again. No answer. The third time she called out, he answered, "I'm here."

The car was destroyed. It lay on its side in such a way that I was the only one who could get out. My mother encouraged me to get out and get help. To do this I had to climb through a broken window and up a 135-foot cliff. Somehow during the spectacular dive we'd taken off the mountain my shoes had fallen off. It was raining as I got out of the car barefoot and clawed my way up the now slippery, treacherous cliff. When I reached the road I looked down and saw our horribly crushed car. It was dusk.

I saw some car lights coming down the road. I stood in the middle of the road and waved the oncoming car to a stop. It turned out to be an EMT. I pointed out our destroyed car. The EMT stopped a couple other vehicles, asking their occupants to help. I watched as a few people climbed down to rescue my parents. I only began to cry when I saw both my parents emerge from the car and climb up the cliff. My father's forehead and face were covered with blood. My mother was shaken but looked fine. We were taken to a clinic to get checked out. While we were waiting to be seen there, someone brought me a pair of shoes. Everyone was staring at us. Mom and I were sore all over, and Dad needed stitches on his forehead, which he had cut on the rearview mirror.

After leaving the clinic we went to dinner. One of the diners had to leave because the sight of Dad's forehead nauseated them. I didn't blame him. We were told that the site of the accident was known to be a dangerous place. Just a few weeks prior a whole family had died as their car sailed off the cliff just as we had done.

Mom decided we needed to get home to Ohio ASAP. It seemed like we were immediately on a bus bound for home. It was nighttime. Mom was angry at Dad, faulting him for the accident, and she refused to sit in the front of the bus with him, which meant I had to sit with her in the back. I felt sorry for Dad because he was injured so badly. He was so sad and sorry. But any kind gesture I made toward him was ignored as if I didn't exist. The only positive thing Mom said was that our car, a Chrysler Valiant, had really lived up to its name. As we were riding home in that bus that night, my parents sitting far apart and me next to my mother, all I felt was the anger between them and that I was totally invisible. Exhausted, I fell asleep.

Suddenly I felt something on my neck that woke me up. I looked at my mom. She was asleep. I closed my eyes and again felt a hand caressing my neck. I froze. My heart beat faster. The hand tried to reach down the front of my chest. I turned my head and bit that hand as hard as I could. The pedophile behind me could not pull his hand back because I was biting it so hard. Finally, I let go. My mother slept through all of this.

Mercifully the bus stopped for a bathroom break. The two men behind us got off the bus. My mom woke up, and I told her what had happened. She said we couldn't tell my dad because he would want to punch the guy and he was already banged up. When the two men returned, one of them offered me some popcorn. Mom said, "You stay away from my daughter. People like you go to jail!" I didn't sleep for the rest of the night, and I don't think Mom did either.

Arriving home, my brothers already knew about the car accident. Mom had called them from the road. When she told them the details, though, suddenly I became the person who'd insisted that we go to the scenic turnout. This kind of accusation was typical of Mom; I was often the scapegoat. But because I loved her so much, I would try to find ways to convince myself that she was right. For instance, perhaps because I had a new camera I had caused the whole thing. If I hadn't had the camera to start with, my mother wouldn't have insisted on us stopping and the accident would never have happened.

By the time I was twelve I was pretty good at convincing myself that I was to blame for whatever my mother accused me of. My brothers enjoyed seeing me get blamed for things and I'm sure they thought, *Better her than me!* Feeling guilty, I didn't discuss the accident with anyone outside of our family.

Dad had been working in the South at that time, so soon after we got home he left for Alabama. His scratched face was the only physical evidence that there had been an accident, the drama of which was soon replaced by the excitement of buying a new car. Mom was in charge of buying it, which was a first. My father and my brothers were crazy about cars so the fact that she got to pick out the car was a complete turnaround. We bought a brand-new Plymouth at the local dealership. I think it was the only new car my parents ever bought. Everyone in my family buried these events as though they never happened. Because I accepted the blame for causing the car accident, I believed that my parents' arguing and my molestation on the bus were also my fault. (It is common for child victims of sexual abuse to feel it was their fault.) I buried all this deep in my mind and my family acted like it never happened. My mother took the attitude that the good Lord had saved us, and we needed to be grateful and celebrate the new car. As far as our neighbors knew, we just bought a brand-new car.

So Wassim had been right about the car accident in which I could have died. He also turned out to be correct about my husband. When I met Georges Leclere he was a young reporter for a French TV network who specialized in science. His unexpected career took him to the United Nations, where he became the director of press, video, and television. Through Georges I met the president of France and other dignitaries from around the world. I also enjoyed dressing up and walking down the red carpet for the Emmy Awards Gala among other such events.

Wassim had read things in my palm from my past and my future. He had clearly seen things in it that would later manifest in the outer world. To me it indicated that a road map of my life existed, and he had access to it. *But how had he been able to discern the plan for my life?* This experience sparked my interest to find out how this all works.

Throughout the years I learned that there are planned events in our lives. Events concerning not only life and death and negative experiences, but also positive, joyful events. Although at the time I didn't know how to seek out this information, I did believe that there was a key to it. In the back of my mind there was a thirst to know more. Why didn't I die during that accident? Why did I get molested? Why did I forget such horrible events for so long?

The randomness of life events can leave us feeling like a ball launched into a pinball machine. It starts with us being tossed into play. There is a rush of movement and lights and energy as we are thrust into life! Then we begin to fall, just like the car in my car accident. Uh-oh! But then we are saved! However, just as we are beginning to acclimate to our new environment, we are smacked up again into the heights—like I experienced when I went to study in Paris.

It's invigorating and exciting and scary too. Every time we adapt to a new way of being, we suddenly experience unexpected challenges. While I thoroughly enjoyed Paris, the studies were so hard that at one point I thought I would have to leave. At the same time my mom stopped talking to me. Then—*ding, ding, ding*! Lights flash, and we are celebrated! In the same year I met my future husband, received my master's degree, got married, and conceived my first child! Then we fall again, before once more being smacked up into a completely new place.

It all happens so fast! The energy, the lights, the colors, the excitement, and the fear keep us in coping mode as we're thrust from celebration to fear to anger to despair and back to celebration again. The whole time we struggle to be in charge and sometimes we even feel that we are in charge. That is, until something unexpected happens again.

The ride continues until one day it's game over. Just like that! Our Soul leaves our physical body and we "die." Where do we go, and what was this life all about, anyway?

I have found the answers to these questions by opening up to communicating with the spirit world. Throughout my career as an energy healer and medium, I have been able to access information that has shown me how to navigate through this pinball machine of life with greater ease. Our physical body along with our Soul, spirit guides, past lives, and reincarnation all play a part in our current "game." More specifically, understanding our Internal Rule Book and Chatter Mind, as well as enhancing communication with the spirit world and our spirit guides, can keep us grounded when we are celebrating with bells and whistles or lift us up when we are lost in a seemingly endless freefall.

This book is my attempt to reveal to you what I've learned on my spiritual journey that can help you decode the workings of your incarnation and figure out how to best navigate through your pinball machine lifetime. I invite you to join me in exploring the inner workings of this exciting adventure called Human Life.

Bon voyage! I hope you enjoy the trip!

1

The Soul

LET'S BEGIN WITH THE PREMISE that we all have a Soul. The *Soul* is a spirit that has incarnated into a physical body that it stays with until the body dies. The Soul's only function is to bring counsel to the physical body it incarnates. There are other spirits who come along to help the incarnated Soul and the physical body it has incarnated, but these other spirits don't incarnate into that physical person. They can however affect the physical world directly, which is something the incarnated Soul cannot do. The incarnated soul affects the physical world by manipulating the physical body in which it is incarnated.

A Soul can be considered an island, and for each incarnation, the Soul creates a peninsula that is formulated specifically for the physical body it will incarnate. It is created by taking aspects of some past incarnations and mixing them together. The entire Soul (the island) that holds all the many incarnations will almost be imperceptible to the individual's Soul (the peninsula) incarnated in a physical body. However the entire Soul will have connections and influence on it. This means that our incarnated Soul is a product of all our past lives but only a few may be obvious to us without specific research into the rest.

Our Higher Self

Our Soul is often called our Higher Self because it brings in the pursuit of spiritual purity to redirect the Earth-based goals of the physical human. The Soul is separate from our physical body, and it's the part of us that exists forever. It goes from incarnation to incarnation, changing bodies, personalities, and even gender from lifetime to lifetime. The Soul needs to adjust to every new body it incarnates into, and part of this process involves integrating the good and the bad experiences from past incarnations into every new incarnation. The Soul brings in some of what we experience during these incarnations as baggage for our Soul/physical body union to process. In each case we are given the opportunity to make choices, and hopefully better ones than when the baggage was created. For example the Soul would bring in the memory of the loneliness of a greedy tyrant from a past-life incarnation to influence someone to share their wealth in their current life/incarnation.

Our Soul resides in the spirit world until it agrees to incarnate into a physical body. The spirit world can be thought of as a "cloud" similar to the computer storage cloud only instead of data, it houses Souls' experiences. When we incarnate into a human body we enter into a life on Earth. We choose to be alive and function on Earth in becoming a human being. The Soul connects with a fetus at some time close to birth and then remains with that physical body throughout its life. When the body wears out and reaches its Final Expiration Date, the Soul detaches from it and returns to the spirit world.

When a Soul incarnates into a body it is like a marriage of two independent beings: one physical and the other spiritual. Initially there is a dance between the physical body dictating what's important to it—namely food and protection, survival and reproduction—and the Soul, who is trying to adapt to the physical body and orient it in the direction of its own higher goals. For example, the physical body wants to wolf down a yummy meal and sleep in the sun while the Soul tries to convince it to get up and do something helpful or productive.

Things can get even more complicated because the physical body and the Soul not only have different agendas but also past-life baggage that can pull them in different directions, creating obstacles and confusion. This is where choice comes in. Our conscious mind evaluates all of the information and then acts accordingly. This action can lead to either a happy life or real problems. When the physical body and the Soul are in coherence they can accomplish *anything*. Of course it's not easy for the two to get aligned and work together toward a common goal.

The Soul along with other spirits get to work right away, as they communicate with a physical infant. Often an infant will look into an empty space and begin to smile or laugh. The infant is actually joyfully responding to a spirit who is in what seems to be an empty space. Spirits of relatives of the infant love to play with them in this way.

The personality of a human being is created by the combination of the Soul and the physical body it incarnates as. The current Soul is a product of bits and pieces of many past incarnations, while the physical body it incarnates as also brings in some past-life experiences and adds free will to the mix. The result is a personality that will show up gradually and then continue to evolve and change as the human being grows up and experiences life.

In its efforts to mold its human into a more loving being, the Soul begins to examine the human's automatic choices. Humans love habit because there are no surprises and surprises can be dangerous. Breaking habits that are usually based on personal comfort is a constant effort for the Soul. Doing the same thing every morning feels good, but your Soul will keep reminding you to change that habit for a better way of being. Instead of waking up in the morning and having breakfast in front of the TV, your Soul might convince you to get up earlier and go jogging or perhaps meditate.

In other ways your Soul will nudge you away from self-indulgence to kindness and service. When you've just settled into a comfy hammock for a nap, it's your Soul that convinces you to get up and mow the lawn, play with your five-year-old, or run to the aid of your neighbor who just fell off his ladder.

Fear is the obstacle that prevents human beings from going beyond their comfort zone: *I can't stop that bully from beating someone up because he might turn on me. I can't get involved in that car accident I just witnessed because I might get caught up in a lawsuit. I can't stand up for someone else or even for myself because I might get hurt.* Our Soul patiently nudges us to overcome that "I can't" feeling.

The Soul has a memory of many incarnations and everything that has transpired in them past and present. To the Soul anything is possible. It has successfully embraced all kinds of goals and challenges in the past and will in the future. The ultimate goal of the Soul is to bring out the best in its human partner.

I Am Who I Am

Each lifetime is unique to us individually, and we have one chance to get it right. My personality, the composition of my DNA, my talents, my intelligence, my looks, my preferences, my energy level, and more make me who I am today and who I will be throughout my lifetime. When I die, my Soul is no longer incarnate; the person I was will no longer continue to develop as a physical human being. My Soul, however, just like everyone else's, will continue to live on. It is through that Soul connection that my life experiences will be recorded and therefore available to reference forever. In this way my Soul never dies, and its incarnation experience also "lives" forever because the Soul can communicate in real time with someone who is currently incarnate.

This means that my Soul, as the person I was during that incarnation, will continue to be available to be contacted and will exhibit the same personality and appearance it had when it was incarnate. Any past incarnations would appear as completely different lives with different looks and personalities. The individual incarnations don't all blend together. Each one is as individual as the human it incarnated. When

I first contact a Soul it will initially look like the human being it was at about the time of death. After that initial identification the spirit will look like they are about thirty years old. In this way the Soul of a deceased friend isn't going to appear as a Viking just because in some past life that friend's Soul had incarnated as a Viking.

A bonus for the previously incarnated Soul is that from its new vantage point in the spirit world, the Soul not only can continue to interact with us but can also have a clearer perspective about what's ahead for their still-living relatives and friends. I know this because for over twenty years I've been contacting my clients' deceased relatives and loved ones. Most of the time these are folks I'd never met when they were alive in their physical body. I'm still amazed at all the information and visual identification I receive about someone I don't know and have never met, and this identification has been corroborated by my clients over and over.

The Incarnation Planning Time

Immediately following the death of the physical body, the Soul has the opportunity to travel to the light and begin its life review. The separation of the Soul and its physical body can happen quickly, slowly, or not at all. For example if someone is in a traumatic accident or has a fatal stroke or heart attack, the soul might immediately detach from the physical body and move instinctively toward a bright light, which is our connection with the Creator. Because of the nature of the death the Soul might be confused at first and might even try to avoid the light in order to stay with the physical body. For people who have had a Near Death Experience (NDE) being enveloped in that extraordinary light brings incredible comfort and wisdom. They usually reconnect with their physical body reluctantly. For people who die slowly, there's a trial period of the Soul leaving the body and then returning. This back and forth continues until the Soul completely detaches. This detachment can take more time when someone really doesn't want to die because they have unfinished business. Reasons for avoiding going to the light can include not wanting to leave loved ones behind who are under their care, seeking revenge, or harboring fear of the unknown, or believing they have lived an "evil" life and they fear the potential consequences of that. To encourage someone to go to the light, frequently deceased loved ones appear to the dying person to soften the transition. I have personally witnessed this while I was holding vigil with someone in transition. At the moment of death, the energy seems to change from struggle to peaceful release. This same change from struggle to peaceful release also happens when a lost spirit goes to the light.

In this state of peaceful release, the Soul begins its Life Review. This is a nonemotional process of simply identifying all the choices made in that lifetime. It is the opportunity to see the life choices we have made "naked," or without the usual emotional attachments of defiance, sorrow, or personal justification for what have turned out to be unfortunate choices. Thanks to this sterile review, Souls can understand how a choice could have been better, which, for example can lead them to tell someone who is still alive that they are sorry for mistreating them in that lifetime.

It is at this point that information from the "peninsula" of the present incarnation joins the whole island of the Soul to create a whole new peninsula/Soul for a new incarnation. In this way the Soul of a particular incarnation is not the full Soul but just a part of a much bigger Soul. Certain elements of past lives are retrieved from that larger Soul and put together as the personality, intelligence, and talents in a new incarnation. For example, past-life elements of being a healer and burned at the stake, a victorious First Nation warrior, a queen defending her castle, and a prostitute could all be put together in the body of a man who, in his next incarnation will champion women's rights internationally and probably never realize why he feels so strongly about this topic.

Although it seems that the full Soul/Island is not present during each incarnation, it really is. We always have access to all the past lives experienced by our full Soul. Just as some people might live on a peninsula and believe that it's an island unto itself, disconnected from the main island and any of the other peninsulas, we humans might believe that our current incarnation is our only one and that there are no past or future lifetimes extending beyond it that we can connect to. The reality is that this connection and therefore access to past-life experiences is always available to everyone but doesn't become obvious without some active discovery. We will look into the influence of a past life on a current incarnation later on.

During the Incarnation Planning Time our spirit or Soul is free of any physical attachment. It has already had many past lives and will create, together with the Creator or benevolent higher power who helped us review our incarnation, a new life based on the particular lessons the individual Soul needs to learn. It's during this time when, depending on what transpired in the last incarnation, a new personality is molded and a suitable physical body is chosen as the incarnation vehicle. Every incarnation is an education with specific characters and events that are designed to help the Soul achieve its goals. Navigating through what we believe are random encounters and events, we have free will where we can choose if and how to respond to the stimuli around us.

Our Soul begins its next incarnation by setting spiritual goals. The goals are a result of our successes and failures in our most recent past life and broadly speaking, often are designed to ensure that we become a nicer, more benevolent person. The Soul has its own unique life plan based on these spiritual goals that it follows every time it connects to a human body. This is a combination of challenges or learning experiences and rewards that help to teach the human how to become a more civilized, kind being.

As such, our Soul is full of ideas and enthusiasm to incarnate and faces amazing challenges to advance spiritually. "Why sure, I can manage this incarnation as a paraplegic," our Soul might say. "Or perhaps cancer would be a great way to face and conquer fear. How about having abusive parents? Or better yet, maybe I'll be an orphan and as such, will experience living in various foster homes. Why not?" The Soul, depending on its past-life experiences, is ready to push the envelope and move rapidly toward the goals of the incarnation at hand. Of course, every Soul has its own challenges, with its long memory of many past lives containing so many wins and losses, but the Soul can look at all this unemotionally and with gusto.

Karma, often expressed as what goes around comes around, also affects our new incarnation by factoring in unpleasant encounters to help us learn our lessons. When we think of karma as punishment, we sometimes feel that we deserve it. That negative emotional charge is counterproductive for our incarnation experience. Rather than think in terms of having done something wrong in a past life therefore we deserve punishment, it's better to not put an emotional charge on negative events. Generally, because identifying karma can be so tricky, rather than assume that any negative experience in our lives is happening to pay back karma, it is better to consider every experience as a *learning* one. Whenever something unpleasant happens to me, I immediately try to understand what I'm supposed to learn from it.

Journey Work

To visit a past life I take my clients on a "journey." This is similar to guided meditation with the addition of bringing my client up to a higher vibration where they can receive spiritual information directly. I accompany my client, but I make sure that I'm a witness to their experience where they describe to me what they perceive. I don't suggest anything about a past life. My job is to make my client feel safe and bring up their vibration to enable them to perceive and verbalize the information they are getting. My clients don't feel negative emotions when we do this work. (Names have been changed to protect their identity.)

A Visit to the Incarnation Planning Time

Neil, a client of mine, had the following experience when we journeyed to his Incarnation Planning Time. We began by first journeying to

Neil's last incarnation before the current one. In that past life Neil described himself as a young Native American man. He was happy, and he loved to canoe on the lakes. He said it was 1842, and he was an Ojibway Indian living in what we now call Minnesota. He had a mother and father as well as an older brother and a younger sister.

In the course of that past life Neil as a very young man, went to work for a white family with two children. The mother wore purple ribbons in her hair. He mentioned that she was always asking him to do things for her. She was very attractive but manipulative and demanding. I asked Neil if anyone reminded him of someone in his current life. He said his native mother, father, and sister reminded him of his present-life family. The woman with the purple ribbons reminded him of his ex-wife.

In the past life Neil and the woman with the purple ribbons had an affair. He had completely succumbed to her seduction and manipulation. When her husband found out, he left her. Neil, abused by this woman in his past life, soon developed a drinking problem. His alcoholism became so acute that it prevented him from functioning, and the woman with the purple ribbons sent him away. Horribly depressed and unable to rejoin his tribe, Neil drank himself to death in that life. On observing his passing, Neil found incredible peace. He relished this after the drama of his past life. He enjoyed this so much it was difficult to get him to the next step.

Finally we proceeded to the Incarnation Planning Time. This began with a review of Neil's past life where he witnessed all his choices. He saw these as colors. When I asked him about this he announced that the color green was missing. This seemed to upset him. I suggested that green is the heart chakra color. He said no, the green was for Mother Earth. I asked him if there was a shape to all the colors. He said that looking at them was like looking into a valley.

He then noticed that green was on the left. That seemed to relieve him a great deal. I tried to move Neil along to the next step, the actual planning, but he was totally engrossed in reviewing these decisions he had made in that past life. Neil noted that he was conducting the review alone; however, he did sense an entity near him. He described this as a bright light that felt good and comfortable. Neil never demonstrated any emotion while he was reviewing the choices he had made in that past life. It seemed that he was simply reviewing data.

However, after reviewing his past life for a long time, so engrossed that he couldn't communicate anything to me except to mutter, "Reviewing," Neil suddenly announced emphatically, "I want a do-over!"

"A do-over?" I questioned him.

"Yes, I want to come back!" he declared. His enthusiasm surprised me. I asked him if he was involved in the choice of participants or events in this new incarnation. He said, "No, I just want to go back." He said this as though he had identified bad choices he had made in that past life, and now he wanted to relive this past life to make better choices. He would enter this new incarnation with trust and enthusiasm. Without me asking, Neil wanted to return because he had goals he wanted to reach. These included better communication, feeling more with his heart, and being more connected to Mother Earth.

We journeyed on to his birth in his current incarnation. I asked Neil when he joined the fetus. He answered that it was sometime close to the moment of birth. He said that he hovered around the fetus first and then they united. At birth Neil was disappointed in his current incarnation. It was not the Native American surroundings he had expected.

Instead everything was moving too fast and there were too many people. Perhaps for this reason Neil's early childhood seemed empty. It wasn't that his parents were mean or that he lived in a bad environment; there was just something missing for him. When Neil agreed to reincarnate, he thought he would return to his happy First Nation life. Instead he found himself in a totally different setting. He never really felt happy in his current incarnation until he was about eight years old and discovered canoeing when visiting his uncle in Canada. Neil said his life changed from that moment on. He became happy!

To this day, Neil finds great joy and comfort through canoeing. I asked Neil if anyone in his past life reminded him of his uncle. He answered, yes, the chief. Another connection between Neil's past life and current incarnation is alcoholism. In the past life Neil had succumbed to alcoholism. In his current incarnation Neil had been an alcoholic but after many years was able to get sober. Apparently Neil also had another opportunity to work things out with the woman with the purple ribbons who had returned as his wife, but rather than allow her to dominate and abuse him, he had been strong enough to leave her.

Besides reviewing our past life in the Incarnation Planning Time, we basically have to agree to reincarnate. We understand the poor choices we have made, and we embrace the idea of a "do-over." We are not really privy to the selection process of who will be in our life again or what the circumstances of our incarnation will be. Remember how Neil wanted a do-over and then was horribly disappointed to find himself in a totally different environment? In the same way, we agree to face challenges that can be reflective of our past life, but how it all will play out is unknown to us.

This is for two main reasons. First of all, we don't have the capacity to orchestrate all the details of a life including the participants. Left to our own devices we would choose the people who we really loved and got along with well rather than those whose presence seemed to be the bane of our incarnation. The latter scenario provides the necessary challenges regarding forgiveness and love. The second reason is that not all of our incarnation is planned beforehand; we have free will to some extent that allows us to make decisions in real time and change the quality of our incarnation. It is true that the highlights of our incarnation are already written and that certain events will happen no matter what. For example, the car accident where my parents and I drove over a cliff and my marriage to Georges are two significant events that were predestined, as were our children. It is tricky to know exactly what is predestined and what is a result of free will. The visual I get of this is an immense three-dimensional mosaic with the individual pieces constantly in motion. Each of us is a piece in that mosaic. As with any mosaic, when you move one piece all the others are affected.

The Creator or some benevolent higher power incorporates appropriate members of our Soul group to incarnate with us. These roles can include those of our parents, our siblings, our significant others, and our children. It also includes people who we believe we have met randomly, although these meetings were planned. The plans for our incarnation also include where we will be born, what our sex will be, what we will look like, and finally a few of the major positive events, people, and of course, challenges that will color our life. Again, all of these are chosen in order to help us achieve the spiritual goals we have agreed to. This is why the people in our lives can be quite dreadful. *How did I get her for my mother?* you might ask, or *Why do I have an uncle who treats everyone so poorly?* Again, our interactions with these various characters teach us to become better people.

Sometimes, however, it takes unbelievably disastrous situations to force us to change and grow. We can be born in a war-torn country or one ravaged by drought and poverty. We might be born suffering from physical challenges or be the member of a minority in a racist country. We could be born one gender and need to switch our sexual orientation during our incarnation. Additional challenges could include severe illness, accidents, a major loss of some sort, physical or emotional abuse— really any kind of adverse event that life can throw our way.

The opposite is also true. We might have magical parents and loving siblings and wonderful significant others as well as outstanding children. These positive events and people can make our whole incarnation worthwhile as we experience love in all its forms—mentally, spiritually, emotionally, physically, and socially.

Many of us have experienced having a relative who acts like a sister to us, or perhaps a daughter who acts like a mother to us. I can remember my younger daughter, Talia, from the time she could talk watching me carefully and pointing out if I wasn't eating. She was constantly concerned about whether I was okay. I often felt that she had been my mother in a past life. My older daughter, Tania, automatically mothered her younger brothers Tristan and Terence, although I was always there with them. It seems obvious that she had been their mother in a past life. When we incarnate there are always a few from the same group of spirits who show up over and over again. Similar to my experience, people have told me that they felt their child must have been their mother in a past life or some other kind of a switch in roles. Odds are, they're correct. Or, as in Neil's case, they replay the same roles.

Some of these past-life experiences and the characters that populate them have been very positive, but not all. In fact, it is the spirits with whom we most need to work things out that often are the most problematic relationships of our lives. My personal favorites are the spirits with whom we've shared wonderful incarnations. In past lives they've been there to take care of us and love us in different ways. These familiar spirits can appear in our current life as we need them. Their arrival and purpose is planned, although beyond the instinct that tells us that this person is familiar, we don't consciously remember any previous incarnations with them.

In my previous book, *Seeing the Dead, Talking with Spirits*, I recounted my transformational yet painful encounter with Foxes, a shaman who taught me about the aura and how to build personal energy. He also taught me how painful it is to give away your energy. I wondered why Foxes had entered my life. I did some personal past-life regressions, and I discovered some of the past lives we had together. Foxes was scheduled to appear in my present incarnation to shake me up and teach me how to work with energy. We were not supposed to work together for long, and we didn't. Foxes did impact my life, and I did learn a lot about energy, which transformed my life in a positive way.

Another surprising past-life encounter happened when as a TV producer I needed the help of an attorney. Someone gave me Fred's phone number. When I called him up to make an appointment, I was filled with overwhelming lust as soon as I heard his voice. This had never happened to me! *Lust? From a voice on the phone? Ridiculous!* I thought. I met with Fred and in the brief meeting I was again overwhelmed with lust! I left the meeting quite confused. A few weeks later I needed to meet with Fred again on business.

As soon as I walked into his office the mutual attraction was palpable. We decided to have lunch. At lunch we didn't even bother to discuss our mutual attraction, but we jumped right away into what we should do about it. Fred was happily living in the suburbs with his wife and children. I was happily living in a different suburb with my husband and children. Regardless of the blatant attraction we had for each other we agreed that in a past life we had enjoyed a very happy relationship but that in our present incarnation there was no room for us as a couple. So many lives around us would be damaged. It seems that once that mutual decision was made, the lust subsided and we completed my business. I didn't need further legal help at that point, and when I did in the future, I turned to a different attorney.

Not only is this an example of a past-life reunion, but it is also an example of free will in our lives. Fred and I could have had an affair and might even have divorced and married each other. If we had, we would have caused a huge amount of confusion and pain to so many innocent people. I'm so grateful that my Soul and spirit guidance prevailed.

So life can be a roller coaster of amazingly wonderful and incredibly awful events and people coming at us in rapid succession, or often all at the same time. Remember the analogy of the pinball machine? The swings of the flippers are intentional.

There is a method to the madness of life. This can be very comforting. The mother of my client Millie committed suicide in front of her when she was a child. Millie, now in her sixties, spent a lifetime trying to understand how something so horrendous could happen to her. When she learned that we agree to the circumstances of our incarnation, including horrendous events, she found great solace in knowing that she had agreed to live this drama. There were lessons that both she and her mother needed to learn from that experience. The idea that she may never know the exact reason why she needed to experience such horror didn't matter. Just knowing that she had agreed to live it empowered her to realize that in some way she was in control.

During this planning time prior to our incarnation, we also establish the date that our physical body will die. This may not happen on the exact date, but it will definitely transpire a few weeks before or after it if it doesn't occur on the actual date itself. This is called the Final Expiration Date. We also have Potential Exit Points where we could die. We set these up to use if we feel that life's challenges are just too much and we need to get out sooner than expected. People who have had a near-death experience (NDE) attest to completely leaving their body and going to the light. Once they are in the incarnation review period, they have a brief opportunity to change their mind and return to their body.

Many autobiographies have been written by people who have experienced NDEs. One of these is by Anita Moorjani, who was dying of cancer in an ICU. Her family was gathered around her to say goodbye as her organs shut down. Anita recounts how she went to the light and then returned to her body. Among the many things she learned was that she had been living her life in fear and that if she returned to her incarnation she would recover from cancer. She now is completely healed and lives a fearless life teaching others what she has learned.

A Past Life with a Near-Death Experience

Agnes was a client of mine who needed to do some past-life work.

Our goal was to go to Agnes's last incarnation before the present one. She first saw an old brick building, like a monastery that was part of or near a castle. We later identified this as being in the mountains between Italy and France. We also identified the year as 1124. Agnes was a twenty-four-year-old man wearing clothes of the era. He was in charge of some important religious scrolls. He knew how to read and write. There were also beautiful drawings in the scrolls that seemed to hold words of the Bible. Agnes, who we will call Auguste, was in charge of the scrolls. He had been left at this monastery when he was two. Auguste was of the nobility but he had been dropped off at this location for his own safety. His father had gone to the Crusades and died. His mother remarried and lived in a castle somewhere else. At twenty-four, Auguste was in charge of the whole place but especially those valuable scrolls. This was his duty, and he had to forfeit any pleasure in the execution of it.

One day a rival, who had a master key to the monastery, got in and stabbed Auguste in the side. The attacker was wearing a white breastplate with a red cross. (From a photo, Agnes identified him as one of the Knights Templar.) It seemed that Auguste had died. He went to the light, and I was waiting to hear about his life review when Agnes said, "There is no life review." I was surprised. Agnes went on to say in an excited voice that Auguste was going to survive his attack.

In fact, it seems that Auguste experienced an NDE. He had gone to the light but once there, he had the option to change the perspective of his incarnation. With the new perspective his Soul would be better equipped to get Auguste through his difficult life fraught with deceit and betrayal. This stronger Soul perspective would call the shots and be completely in charge. The former weaker perspective Soul would still exist, but not dominate Auguste's personality.

Auguste returned to his body, but now he was ruthless. Agnes described with horror how Auguste burned down a village including the inhabitants. She recoiled at how coldly he could do this. It was as though he had turned into a monster. He had no empathy for anyone. He knew he was royalty and conducted himself in that manner, simply accepting the social order. In fact, Auguste's new Soul perspective had taken over the physical part of this incarnation.

We moved forward to the next event in that past life. Auguste was now a very tired old man. He had a marriage of convenience with a smart woman who respected him and bore him seven children. Auguste had no love connection with his children or his wife. The last event *in his life was to visit a woman in a turret of his structure. He was attracted to her. It was the only time he was attracted to anyone. He went up to the turret, but he did not have an affair with her because it would interfere with his duties. It would be a distraction.*

When it came time for Auguste to pass, he saw a dark door but didn't want to go through it. This seemed to be the entrance to death. A long arm came out of the doorway and pulled him in. As he passed through the doorway he seemed to return to who he had been in his youth. He regretted that he had been so bound by duty. He felt he had missed a lot in life. He had seen servants as invisible. He had killed many people, but he believed this was necessary to gain respect and order. He had never allowed himself to experience love. His one opportunity was the woman in the turret, but he declined that relationship to stay true to his duty.

Agnes's spirit was appalled at Auguste's callous nature. In the Incarnation Planning Time it seems Auguste had no input. He was not asked if he wanted to incarnate again. He simply knew he had to do it. No choice. Agnes didn't recognize anyone from that past life as being in her current incarnation with the exception of her father, who might have been a monk in that past life.

In her present incarnation Agnes described how she had been a bit brutal as an infant and a child. When she was six months old, she would hit her parents in the head with her bottle when she wanted it filled. As a nine-year-old, she was large and was feared by her classmates after a bully tried to hurt her, and she beat up the bully and anyone else who tried to tease her. It was only when she went through puberty that she decided she wanted to act like a gentle girl.

We are all finely cut diamonds with many facets. As we mature there is one face that dominates the others. Agnes, as Auguste, had an NDE, which showed her that she had the strength within herself to persevere and conquer. In her current incarnation, Agnes realized that she was better off showing a milder, kinder self.

Our Soul is in charge of accomplishing the goals of a new incarnation. Many people who are authorities on meditation tell us that we have all the answers. I believe that is true. Our Soul has access to all the information we could ever want. We can access this through meditation or communication with our spirit guides. The Akashic Records are believed to contain not only our life plan but absolutely everything that has ever occurred or will occur in our Universe.

Since absolutely all participants, history, and wisdom are available in the Akashic Records, people consult it to better understand the why of some events and gain insight when making decisions. There are practitioners who are specialized in accessing this record.

Our Birth Spirit Guide

To help us in this daunting task of incarnating, we are given a spirit guide at birth, whose job is to watch over both our physical body and our Soul. Our birth spirit guide is different from our Soul and never incarnates into our physical body. The birth spirit guide, chosen during the Incarnation Planning Time, is constantly with us from the moment we are born into our physical body and is a spirit who may have incarnated with us in the past. With it by our side we are definitely never alone and are constantly privy to amazing, nonjudgmental support and unconditional love.

It should also be noted that when we plan the circumstances of our incarnation, our birth spirit guide is merely an observer. It's not allowed to help us plan our life or interfere in it in any way without our specific request, unless we are at risk of dying when it's not our predetermined time to die. This is key to our relationship.

The Soul's purpose is to directly get involved with all of the human's choices.

The Soul does not experience emotions but witnesses those felt by its host. This is one aspect of incarnation that is so daunting for a Soul as it tries to motivate a body drowning in fear or anger to act in a kind and loving way and thus achieve its goals. Another big obstacle for the Soul is the physical body's mind, which collects everything that happens, attaches a value to it, and then uses those values to create a framework to help the physical body survive and thrive. I call this the Internal Rule Book, and we will be exploring it further in the chapters to come.

A human has the capacity to make decisions, so when our Soul makes a suggestion, the human will take action either to follow the suggestion or ignore it. Have you heard the expression "look before you leap"? This refers to the human needing to pay attention to the directives of our Soul. In fact there is a kind of tug-of-war between the goal-oriented influence of our Soul and the simple self-centered survival tendencies of our human self. For instance, two-year-old Tommy sees Jimmy pick up Tommy's favorite truck. The Soul directs Tommy to let Jimmy play with his truck. Instead Tommy runs up to Jimmy, grabs the truck, and then hits Jimmy with it to punctuate his ownership. *That'll teach you to touch something of mine*, Tommy thinks triumphantly. Fortunately our Soul is patient, nonjudgmental, and loving.

Unlike the Soul, the birth spirit guide has less direct influence on its human charge but is able to take action outside the Soul's human body. So if little Becky is pulling the tablecloth off the table and there is a large vase on it that would kill her if it fell on her head, then rather than influencing Becky directly, her Soul would try to convince her to stop and her birth spirit guide could intervene by waking up the sleeping babysitter who then is able to stop the vase from falling on Becky. This kind of intervention can be physical. For example the babysitter could be woken up by physically feeling some nudging on her arm.

Nevertheless, it must be frustrating for our birth guide to watch us ignore our Soul and make mistakes, all the while not being allowed to intervene. Normally the extent to which a birth guide can help us is to encourage us to make decisions in our own best interest. They do this by setting up coincidences or synchronicities for us to experience. Or they put symbols and signs in our path for us to interpret as invitations to go in one direction or another. They are the helpers of our Soul. And again, our birth guide can't help us unless we ask it to, and it will only intervene if our lives are in danger of ending before our Final Expiration Date. As we grow up we also gain other spirit guides to help our Soul and physical body. These other spirit guides can be relatives who passed or other spirits who have proficiency or skills to help us accomplish a task. For example a surgeon might have a spirit who was a successful surgeon in their own incarnation whispering to them.

∾ How to Communicate with Your Birth Guide

The easiest way to establish a line of communication with your birth guide is to do the following:

1. Set aside at least twenty minutes of quiet time in a place where you feel very comfortable and safe.

2. Say a prayer to a higher benevolent power like God. It can be a formal religious prayer or one that you simply make up. I am Christian so I like the Lord's Prayer.

3. Imagine a beautiful light above your head. This is the light of the creator.

4. Now imagine a thread coming down from that beautiful light, entering the top of your head, and descending through your head and down your neck to your heart center.

5. As this light fills your heart center, the light above your head still remains bright and full. Your heart center will begin to fill up with that beautiful light, and you will feel like it's radiating out. You become like the sun where nothing negative can get to you.

6. Keep your eyes closed and ask the name of your birth guide. The first name that comes to mind is your birth guide's name. Just accept it.

7. Try to identify how you perceived that name. Did you hear it inside or outside your head? Did you imagine it written? This determines whether you're best form of communication with your birth guide is hearing or seeing.

8. Continue your communication with your birth guide. Trust that you received the right information.

A Spirit Guide Deals with Death

I was driving home from Manhattan into the suburbs. It was after 11:00 p.m. as I drove through the sleepy town where I lived. As I was approaching a five-corner crossroads where the light was green, a car came speeding up behind me on my left. I swerved to my right to avoid getting hit by the car that was speeding by, but unfortunately I drove right into a telephone poll. When I regained consciousness, I found that my airbag had blown up.

I got out of the car to survey the damage. There was no one around that late at night. Once I saw how badly the car was damaged I decided I needed to call someone. I was reaching for my car door when I heard the words, "Don't touch that door! There are live wires on the car." I turned toward the voice and saw a man standing in the shadows. I again looked at the car and sure enough there were live wires dangling on it. I turned to look at the man again, and he was gone. Before I knew it the police and an EMT arrived, but there was no one else on the scene. How had that man disappeared so fast? I believe that one of my spirit guides had appeared to save my life.

Another case where I felt one of my spirit guides intervene was when I was walking my dog at night and was about to cross the street. The light was in my favor and as I took a step forward, I looked to my left to see a car driving up at full speed, despite the red light in front of it. I had my weight on my right foot moving forward, so all I could do was lean back quickly. But all of a sudden I was flying several feet backward and landing on the ground. Meanwhile, the driver, after missing me by mere inches, had stopped his car to help lift me up from the ground.

I think I got a better lift from my spirit guide!

And of course there's the car accident I had when I went over that cliff with my parents. I'm sure that one of my spirit guides was there, *helping me to scramble up that wet, crumbling mountainside and hail a passing car.*

Discretion is key to the job of the birth guide and any other spirit guides who join us. Except for an untimely death, no heavy-handed intervention is allowed, even though our decisions can make us miserable. All our birth guide or spirit guides can do is provide tissues for us as we cry or drop a self-help book or magazine in front of us, hoping it will get our attention, and we will pick it up and read it.

A birth guide can have a specialty point of view. My birth guide has helped me care about my looks of all things. I often communicate with her, and she with me. Some days, when I have no idea what to wear and I ask her advice, I'll remember a piece of clothing I'd forgotten all about. She'll have me rummaging through my closet to find it. She also puts together outfits that I normally wouldn't consider wearing.

I used to wonder why I have the birth guide I do. She is wonderful, and I love her very much. She is brave and encourages me at just the right time. Her interest in how I look is based on my critical self-image. With her help I feel really good about myself, as we all should feel about ourselves and I give myself the care that is so important to all of us. Communicating with your birth guide will definitely improve your life in unexpected ways.

Angels, Other Spirits, and Spirit Guides in Our Lives

As I mentioned above, in addition to our birth guide who is present with us from birth, we also have other spirit guides or simply spirits around us. As we go through life, a whole variety of spirits and spirit guides join us to help, observe, or distract us in a good way. When we need help on a project or in our career, spirit guides who are specialized in that particular field will circle around us, offering us suggestions. There are also spirits of loved ones who have died or other random spirits.

Many people consider all spirits, including loved ones who died, to be angels. But technically angels are spirits that never incarnated. Because each person develops a belief system through personal lived education and experience, and this belief system can vary a great deal from one person to another, it is important to not get caught up with labels. In other words if you want to call spirits angels, go for it. Comfort is the key to spirit communication; if you feel comfortable and trust your angel or spirit guide experience, it can be amazingly helpful in your life.

At the Mediumship Group meetings that I run, I often see spirit helpers around the meeting participants. When I identify some of them it sometimes turns out that the participant is working in a field that's of interest to the spirit helper. For example, next to April, one of the group's participants, I saw the spirit of a strong woman who looked like she was from the 1800s by the way she was dressed. I described her to April. It turned out that April was writing a play about that woman. I guess her spirit wanted to make sure April got it right.

Around Gail I described a spirit with long blonde hair. Gail asked me if her name was Dolores.

"Yes," the spirit told me.

"Who is Dolores?" I asked Gail.

"She was my best friend who died way too soon," Gail explained. It was obvious that Dolores had never completely left her best friend.

These spirits can help us achieve our goals when we ask for help. In this, they help us to make the most out of who and where we are. They are constantly making suggestions and putting new ideas in our minds and trying to bring us a better perspective about our issues. When we're in a rut, we generally ignore these noble efforts by immediately discounting them: *I could never do that! That's too expensive! That's too risky! Not for me! I couldn't possibly . . . !*

Most often fear keeps us from venturing out and trying something new. Part of this is due to our Internal Rule Book, which we will learn more about in chapter 2. The Internal Rule Book records in our subconscious mind everything that happens to us and adds a value judgment to it.

Because of spiritual past-life events and our Internal Rule Book we become like a dog within an electric fence. A failed attempt at something serves as the electric shock of that "fence." Similar to the Journey Work I use for past-life regression, I use it to turn off the current and disarm the fence. In so doing we can hear our Soul, birth spirit guide, and all the other helpful spirits informing us as to what to do. They embolden us to venture forth and try new things. During the Journey Work I can empower my client to make choices in their own best interest.

In my book *Seeing the Dead, Talking with Spirits* I write about how I became aware of my spirit guide Tatonka, a Lakota elder, and how he affected my life by encouraging me to get involved with Lakota ceremonies. This has become an important part of my life; it really grounds me. Spirit guides vary according to our needs. Tatonka came to me to help when I was a sickly child. Without being aware of his presence, he taught me to be brave and how to thrive. He became apparent to me only when I was much older and ready to start a new chapter in my life.

Other spirit guides appear to help facilitate healing. Some of them appear whenever I begin a session, while others appear with my client, meaning that they travel with that client or are somehow connected with them. What I find interesting is that people are so quick to attribute breakthrough ideas to inspiration when it is really a spirit guide whispering guidance. In our society we are hesitant to acknowledge the existence of a spirit world or spirits in general. This is truly unfortunate because we are apt to miss so much.

The Spirits and the Universe Align

We have free will to make decisions about the actions of our physical body within the context of destined events. For example, I can decide to get up at 7:00 a.m. My Soul can decide that I should wake up at 5:00 a.m. The result may be that I wake up suddenly at 5:00 a.m. but I don't get out of bed. It's my choice to get up and out of bed or just lie there for another couple of hours.

I control my body—until I don't. Suddenly I need to pee. Again, it's my choice to get out of bed, but the consequences aren't pretty if I stay in bed. Or perhaps my Soul engages the help of a spirit to get the cat to knock down the large vase full of flowers in the kitchen. Crash! What's the point of this kind of interference in my life? Perhaps a predestined event was going to happen at a certain time, and I needed to get up at 5:00 a.m. to be ready for it. Our Soul has a bigger picture of our life and has the job of getting us to the right place at the right time to benefit from that predestined event.

In the same vein, when we are headed in the wrong direction, our Soul, working with our spirit guides, will adjust things around us to ensure that things happen in a certain way. This is similar to driving somewhere and getting green lights the whole trip, or red lights as the case may be. The following is an example from my own life.

Looking for Romance

After I graduated from college I was working for a senator in Washington, DC. My goal was to earn money to go to Paris to get my master's degree at the University of Paris, at the Sorbonne. While I was in Washington, DC, I met David, who was a junior in college. He was participating in a work/study program that was fostered by Northeastern University. David wanted to become an attorney so he worked for the Justice Department in DC as part of this program. We hit it off and in no time we had become a couple. Having saved enough money to then go to Europe, it seemed that far too soon the date of my departure for France was approaching.

I went home to Ohio to pack, and David returned to Massachusetts. After hours on the phone David surprised me with a trip to my home. I was planning to leave in July to travel with a friend through Europe and then end up in Paris to study in the fall. International communication back then was complicated. There were no cell phones, and phone calls were expensive and would be difficult to arrange. Our lifeline was the mail. Thus, as you might imagine, this made it very *tricky to communicate, both for the sender and the receiver.*

The way correspondence took place was to address mail to an American Express (Amex) office in a large city. If you were an Amex cardholder, your mail would be held for a week. My travel friend was very organized in this regard. Falcon, a nickname of my travel partner, figured out the dates that a letter would need to be mailed to arrive in an Amex office in whatever country we would be visiting at the specific time we would be there. This information included the date by which a letter needed to be mailed to coincide with our arrival in that city. I gave this information to my family and David and tearfully he and I said goodbye, promising to write each other.

My trip to Europe was amazing, and I loved every bit of it! Falcon had organized the whole trip, and I just followed along. Every day I wrote David a letter and in every big city Falcon and I went to the Amex office to pick up our mail. Falcon always got some mail. I never got any mail. This made me feel terrible! I had communicated the same exact dates, but I got no mail. I wasn't surprised that I hadn't received any mail from my family. My parents were scheduled to meet me in Europe.

But David? I was heartbroken! As I continued the trip, however, my heart began to heal. I found reasons why David wasn't really someone I wanted to be with. I'd be in Paris, a great place for starting a new life. Gradually the pain of his rejection softened and was replaced with the excitement of that new life. Falcon flew back to the States for medical school. In Rome I met my future Paris roommate, Kate, and we spoke of the studies and lives we individually were planning.

It seemed that anything was possible, and David would only have put a wrench into the works by keeping me attached to him in the States. The last city I visited before meeting my parents was Munich. There I went to the Amex office for the mail, but I really was doing that more out of habit than anything else. How surprised I was when I found a letter from David's mother!

She wrote me that David was very upset because all the letters he had written to me had been returned to him by Amex. This bothered him so much that he decided to go to Germany to meet me! The day he had planned to meet me was that very day! I was bewildered. Kate and I spent the day visiting Munich and then returned to the youth hostel where we were staying. David was waiting outside, with all of the many letters that had been returned to him.

I was surprised by my lack of enthusiasm to see him, and he was too. My parents were due to arrive the next day, and I was scheduled to travel with them. David, a great romantic, decided that he and I would meet again a month from that day on top of the Eiffel Tower at 3:00 p.m.

It turned out that David had also registered to study at the Sorbonne that year. We did meet at the top of the Eiffel Tower! We continued to date, but it was a rough year. We just couldn't seem to achieve the level of closeness we'd enjoyed before. When we said goodbye the last time, it really was forever. I had another year in Paris to complete my degree, and David had another year to receive his bachelor's.

When I reflect on my relationship with David it seems obvious to me that my Soul, spirit guides, and the Universe definitely didn't want us to stay together. It's as though a large network of spirits delayed my mail from David while allowing Falcon to receive mail. If I'd received those romantic letters, they certainly would have kept the flame of love alive in my heart. David and I surely would have married. But it wasn't meant to be.

My incarnation planning had something else in mind for me.

I began another year of study at the Sorbonne. After a few months, I met Jean François, who was studying architecture. He was handsome, studious, and fun. He had a friend named Jean Pierre and he and Kate and Jean François and I would often go out together. It soon became obvious that Jean François and I were a couple. Life seemed great! Then one day Jean François told me he was engaged. I was shocked and hurt. How could he be dating me while engaged to someone else? He told me this before a holiday, when he was returning to his home in Nevers where he said his fiancée lived.

Rather than wallow in self-pity, I threw myself into my work. My thesis was a comparison of the pressures on news broadcasting in the United States and France. I had done my research in the States and now needed to do the research in France. To do this I needed to interview some French reporters. With my newly gained energy wherein I believed that "the only thing left for pitiful me to do is finish my master's," I boldly marched into one of the three state-run French TV stations. With no problem at all, I spoke to one of the network heads. He was delighted to put me in contact with the national news reporters who I needed to talk to in order to conduct my research.

It all seemed to flow effortlessly. Soon enough I was in a room full of national news reporters who were feeding me lots of information about their work. At one point a good-looking young man entered the room and discreetly went to make a phone call. The phone system in France at that time was antiquated. Not only was it practically impossible to get a phone in your home, many of the phones that did exist could only be used in central Paris.

I heard this attractive man call his mother and ask, in Russian, whether his laundry was ready. I found this was too funny. I turned to him and spoke to him in Russian. He gave me his card—his name was Georges Leclere—and asked for my phone number. The only number I had was that of the stained-glass company where I worked part-time, which I gave him.

Georges called me every day for a week before I agreed to go out with him. The moment I did, we immediately fell in love. Although his English was awful and my French certainly needed improvement, it felt like we had known each other forever, and we became inseparable for two weeks. Then he left on a business trip for a month. During that time I didn't date anyone else. When we were together again it was as if we'd just seen each other the day before. We decided to get married. Five months later we had our formal wedding in Ohio. Everything had happened so effortlessly.

From the spiritual perspective I have today, I believe that Georges and I were destined to marry. First, however, the universe needed to remove David and Jean Pierre from the scene. It was perfect timing for Spirit to send Georges into the conference room where I was with the group of reporters and call his mother in Russian! As for Jean Pierre, after his vacation he came over to my apartment just like he'd always done, unannounced, and expected me to go out with him. Georges and I were on our way out, and Jean Pierre was furious to see me with someone else. He stayed after Georges and I left and fumed to Kate about how cavalierly I had dumped him.

When Kate tried to explain that I wouldn't date someone who was engaged, Jean Pierre said that he'd never actually been engaged! He had told me that lie because he was afraid that our relationship was moving too fast. I can just imagine a spirit whispering to Jean Pierre that he should tell me he was engaged because we were getting too close. It certainly was effective in breaking us up.

Animals and Spirits

Everything and everyone has spirit energy attached to it in some form or another. Human beings have the most developed form of Soul and body connection. This has to do with the more advanced mind of a human. What we would call "intelligent animals" also have Souls and spirits. It is a frightening prospect for a Soul to incarnate. Because of this, a Soul might practice incarnating into a cat or dog. The level of goals is limited by the sheer physical possibilities of the animal. Nevertheless animals have impressed us with heroic acts of bravery. These come from the animal's Soul encouraging it to rise above its basic animal desire to survive, thrive, and reproduce.

In the Incarnation Planning Time it is possible for a Soul to transition from incarnating as a dog or horse to a human being. Here are a few stories from my therapeutic work that illustrate this point.

A Horse Is a Horse, of Course, of Course!

Kerrie was an exceptionally beautiful and intelligent young woman. She went to an Ivy League school and graduated with high honors. Her wealthy parents doted on her, their only child, and Kerrie grew up surrounded by love and enjoying the best things that life could offer. In her early twenties, Kerrie fell in love with Jason. Even though none of her friends really liked him, the two became a couple, but they never were happy. Jason was a nightmare boyfriend to Kerrie. To her friends' amazement, Kerrie continued to take a lot of abuse from Jason. She seemed to spend all her time crying.

It was Jason who finally broke up with Kerrie. She was inconsolable. In desperation Kerrie came to see me. She didn't understand her attachment to Jason, given how badly he'd treated her. During our Journey Work Kerrie saw a wild horse that she was trying to tame. For some reason she became obsessed with breaking this horse, but she never succeeded. I asked Kerrie what she was supposed to learn from that past life. She said that it was very bizarre, but the horse was Jason. Not Jason in a symbolic way. No, it really was Jason in a past life. Jason never had another girlfriend, and he continued brooding about Kerrie his entire life. One day he committed suicide.

I believe that Jason remembered Kerrie from his previous incarnation, and he couldn't let go of his resentment and anger toward her for treating him so poorly. On top of this Jason was miserable during his current incarnation because it was so much more complicated being a human being than a horse. He had many more choices to make, and he was so overwhelmed by them that he finally ended his life.

A Big Fish in a Small Pond

Kenneth wanted to find out his most influential past life, so we began our Journey Work. Kenneth was proceeding well as we approached the moment when he stepped into the light to observe his past life. Rather than quickly beginning to describe something, Kenneth was suddenly silent. When this happens I encourage my clients to describe anything that comes to mind. I find it helpful to ask them what they have on their feet. But Kenneth had no answer. He did, however, begin to describe where he was.

"It's really hot. I seem to be on a rock."

I encouraged Kenneth to see what else he observed.

"Lizard. I hear the word lizard! Wait a minute! I don't have feet! I am a lizard!"

"You were a lizard in that past life?"

"Yes, but not just a lizard. I was the Lizard King!"

As surprising as this might seem, knowing Kenneth and his dislike of large groups and timid personality, it made sense that he might have been a lizard in a previous life. In that past life Kenneth's Soul felt emboldened as he was King of the Lizards. A big fish in a small pond. Incarnating into a human was a bigger pond than he had anticipated and that's why he had so much trouble adjusting to his human incarnation. Kenneth was pleased with his past life where he was a powerful king.

Animals Can Channel Spirits Too

Animals will also lend their bodies to be used temporarily by a Soul who had previously been human.

One day I was working with a client and Natasha, my standard poodle, was with me. Usually during a session she sleeps in a corner of the room and waits for us to finish. My client was on a journey where she was meeting her mother who she desperately missed since her passing a few years prior. Suddenly Natasha came forward and, to my horror, started to climb up on the couch with my client. I tried to keep her down, but she insisted on climbing up. My client welcomed Natasha as she stretched out on top of her in a full body hug. The spirit of my client's mother had jumped into Natasha to comfort her daughter. Natasha often accepts a spirit who wants to show affection to a client in this or similar ways.

Fate, Destiny, and
Free Will

When our Soul is in the Incarnation Planning Time, future events are established that will manifest throughout our life. These events can include meeting people to love, getting the perfect job, winning the lottery, buying one's dream house, or having a serious accident, losing a job, failing the bar exam, or contracting a serious illness. These are all life-changing events. There are also coincidences or what some call synchronicities where things seem to magically align.

Sophie's Baby

Sophie was pregnant with her third child. Every pregnancy of Sophie's had been treated by her wealthy parents as the arrival of an heir to a great throne. No one could get better care or attention; only the best would do. Therefore Sophie was quite surprised when she found herself alone in the back seat of her car, painfully giving birth while her husband navigated the traffic jams of Manhattan.

The three of them arrived at the hospital. In her arms, Sophie held her baby, who was still attached to the amniotic sack, which was still inside of Sophie. She and her husband walked into the front entrance of the very fancy New York hospital where Sophie had given birth in high luxury in her past two pregnancies. It seems that Sophie was supposed to experience giving birth to her third child under difficult circumstances, unlike her two previous deliveries, which had been professionally handled and not painful at all.

During the Incarnation Planning Time Sophie's Soul and that of her baby had planned that this would happen. Sophie's challenging experience made her more aware of the many women around the world who give birth under nearly impossible conditions. As a result, she began to financially support organizations that assist childbearing women as well as birthing centers offering prenatal care.

While some things are preplanned, we also have free will, which we may employ to make choices as we wend our way through life. In the movie *Sliding Doors* Gwyneth Paltrow is a downtrodden young woman in London named Helen. She has a miserable job that she hates. She arrives on the platform of a London tube station just as the subway's doors close. Because she misses her train, she doesn't get home in time to witness her boyfriend cheating on her. The boyfriend is a nasty, demanding, lazy bum. He mistreats Helen as she scrambles to support him. Eventually she does catch him cheating on her, and he decides to leave Helen. Very depressed, she hears that a close friend is in the hospital. She rushes over to the hospital and bumps into a man. They fall in love.

The next scene takes place in the same London tube station, but this time Helen makes her train. She arrives home and finds her boyfriend cheating on her. This makes her so angry that she throws her boyfriend out. Although she is very upset, she decides to change her life. She quits the job that she detests and finds another one more to her liking. Generally she is much better off in her new life even though she is still depressed that she doesn't have a boyfriend. Nevertheless, she socializes with friends and has fun. At one point Helen hears that a close friend is in the hospital. She rushes over there and bumps into a man. They fall in love.

So what's the difference between fate and destiny in this scenario?

Fate would be the way Helen's character muddled through life accepting her boyfriend's bad treatment of her, without her having much hope of a better future. Destiny would be the way her character had made the most of the situation she'd found herself in. Rather than muddle along, she quit her job and tried her hardest to find a better one and have fun, all the while hoping to meet someone to love. In both cases the situation of having her boyfriend cheat on her devastated her. In the first scenario she remained depressed and in the second she picked herself up and made the most of her life. In both stories the man she would fall in love with arrived on the scene at the same time.

All of this pertains to the decisions she made about her life that would either keep her in a cage of depression or free her. The depressed Helen could only hear her mind telling her she didn't deserve to be treated better by her boyfriend and that she didn't deserve a better job. The motivated Helen was able to quiet her mind and seek out past moments of success that propelled her into a happier life.

Adding Randomness to the Big Picture

Our physical body learns quickly that our conscious decisions and actions carry consequences for us. What we don't realize is that these consequences are far-reaching and affect everyone and everything around us to some extent. Imagine a three-dimensional mosaic wherein each piece is a person. Every time any person makes a decision, regardless of how big or small it might seem, everything around that person shifts. This keeps the mosaic, and all its various facets, moving all the time. There is energy attached to each decision and consequence, as well as to our every thought.

The election of a president of a country is a good example of an individual decision that affects many people. Just think how often an election is won or lost by a handful of votes. A majority decision to elect a president demands a great deal of energy to attract a candidate's supporters but also to motivate potential voters to actually vote. In this scenario it's easy to identify the moving mosaic quality of people's decisions and actions on each other and on a group, and in some cases even on the world. Our Soul tries to influence our decisions for the benefit of ourselves and society at large.

A Case in Point

One warm Sunday night I was at a barbeque at my son Tristan's home in a quiet residential area. It was a block party atmosphere with neighbors and their children coming and going, filling the street with talk and laughter. The food was great as usual, and the company was fun.

All the guests had left, and it was 9:30 p.m. Time to go home. Just as I was about to walk out the door a client called. Even though I was tired and really just wanted to leave, I answered the call. While I was talking to my client, a truck came racing by and totaled my car. Had I not listened to my Soul and taken that call from my client, I would have been in that hit-and-run accident.

Most of the time we have no idea of the consequences of our decisions. This accident had consequences for the entire neighborhood. All the neighbors united to offer help in any way they could. They told the police about the vehicle, which some of them could identify.

The following day the driver of the truck came forward and took responsibility for the accident. This was a big wake-up call for him. He realized that his carelessness could have severely injured or even killed someone. Also a hit-and-run is a felony in New York, and the driver might have been concerned that he would be found; therefore it was better to fess up and pay for the repairs.

From the Mouths of Babes

For those people who are skeptical about past lives and reincarnation, there is the fascinating example of young children who remember their past lives. In the final episode of a video series called *Surviving Death*, children who have remembered their past lives are interviewed. These declarations are supported by finding the obituary of the deceased person that the child professed to be and then providing the children, aged three to six years old, with choices of photos that were thought to be part of their past life. Intermixed with these photos were others that had nothing to do with the deceased. The child was invited to select the photos that looked familiar to them. The whole process from the identification of the past life to the correct choice of photos is very compelling.

Dominica's Former Home

My client Saria describes how her three-year-old daughter, Dominica, would point out a specific house in their city as her home. The problem was that Saria lived across the city in a whole different neighborhood. Nevertheless every time Saria and her daughter would pass by that house Dominica would point at it and announce that it was her home. At that time Saria and her family had no knowledge about reincarnation and it upset them that Dominica couldn't identify her real home. They would just tell her she was wrong. In retrospect, now that Saria is a healer herself, she wishes that she had been able to interview Dominica to find out more about her previous incarnation. This is typical for parents whose children remember their past incarnation. It is very unsettling for parents who think there is something wrong with their child rather than understanding that this is beautiful proof of how our Soul never dies but morphs into a new incarnation.

❧ 2 ❧
The Body

NOW THAT WE'VE EXPLORED the spiritual side of things, let's take a look at how our physical world works, and how it interacts with our spiritual self.

As mentioned in chapter 1, the Soul joins the physical body when the fetus is about to be born. Here it begins to dialogue with the mind of the new baby and then tries to help the baby override its animal nature. Remember that at the same time the Soul is trying to communicate with its human, that human's mind is registering everything that happens into its Internal Rule Book. Every entry in the Internal Rule Book has a value attached to it. This value is hardwired to human emotions. It takes time for the Soul to navigate through the emotionally charged experiential whirlwind of the Internal Rule Book. This struggle for the Soul will continue throughout the incarnation. As the baby grows up and increasingly takes control of its physical needs—survival, comfort, protection, reproduction—all things physical gradually take precedence over anything or anyone in spirit.

The Trajectory of Our Lives
from Birth On

To begin with, the physical body is chosen specifically to present the Soul with the challenges the Soul needs to progress. It therefore helps turn the physical person into a civilized being. This may include all kinds of physical challenges for an infant to face. At the same time the Soul is not perfect and needs these incarnations for it to develop.

In utero we've had some time to adjust to dealing with a physical body (our own) and the energies and vibrations of the physical world around us. This includes our relationship with our mother.

While it's possible for a fetus to experience distress before birth, for the most part being in a womb is very comfortable. Of course what the mother eats can affect the fetus in a negative way, or something like an umbilical cord around the fetus's neck causes physical stress. There are many ways the fetus can feel uncomfortable in the womb but usually the womb is a place of comfort. Outside the womb is uncomfortable for all babies. Parts of our body can get irritated, we feel hunger, and sometimes the food we're given might make us sick. Remember, comfort equals survival and survival is a full-time job! Meanwhile our Soul tries to influence the fetus by pointing out comforting words or sounds.

Finally, one way or another, we have to leave our mother's womb. Through the impressive experience of vaginal birth or the surprising transition of womb to world at large through C-section, we find ourselves utterly dependent and, although terrified, filled with an innate desire to survive, which is dominated by our search for comfort. If we feel comfortable, we can survive. To get our needs for comfort met, we try all the tricks we can come up with. We kick our legs, scream, cry, smile . . . You get the idea. Gradually we figure out what gets the best results. Our needs include not only food, but also physical nurturing. We need to be held and loved. I believe that this is a transfer of life force energy, which is essential for our physical survival at any age.

Meanwhile, we are physically changing at lightning speed. Perhaps it's not as fast as a colt that stands up right away after being born and trots off with its mother, but we quickly gain some semblance of control over our bodies, and we learn to communicate with those around us.

The proper development and survival of an infant depends on it being fed milk from its mother or formula. Drinking the milk doesn't kill the source of the milk. Later on that child will need to expand its diet by eating food derived from other sources, beginning with ripe fruits and vegetables. Here again, as with the milk, the food source doesn't "die" to produce the food; the plant merely renders its fruits to be eaten. Eventually the child will need to include more protein in its diet, which will include fish and animals. Personal survival is so important that there is never a thought that to obtain the life-sustaining protein, something must die.

Noting this is crucial because this acceptance that something must die so I may live is central to the great challenge that faces a Soul incarnating into a human or animal body. The animal is just as interested in surviving and multiplying as the human is. Left to their own devices a human would only be interested in self-preservation and not care that the animal has sacrificed its life so that the human can eat. The Soul becomes that nudging voice urging the individual to make the decision of compassion and/or personal sacrifice by either recognizing the sacrifice of the animal and thanking it for that sacrifice or perhaps by becoming vegetarian and thus overriding the natural instinct for self-preservation at the expense of another's life.

Communicating with the Spirit World

As we've learned, communication with the physical body is important to the Soul, and the success of a Soul in "taming" its body depends, in large part, on the connection it can develop with that physical body. It's also true that over time the baby will have less and less to do with the spirits around it. As the baby turns into a toddler and then a young child, the innate ability to see, hear, and feel spirits recedes. This allows the child to concentrate on getting its physical needs met. When communication does happen between child and Soul and spirits in general, our caregivers for the most part, unfortunately, ignore it or say that it doesn't exist or worse—that it's dangerous and bad.

My Friend Marilyn

When I was a young child I had an invisible friend whose name was Marilyn. She joined me when my best friend, Janie, moved away and I was very lonely. Marilyn and I had a lot of fun together. We discussed interesting things, and we laughed. She filled my world. Not knowing how to handle this, my mother took me to our family doctor. Joyfully I described Marilyn to him. He told me and my mother that this was very bad, and I needed to immediately stop it! Being an obedient little girl, I said goodbye to Marilyn and made a conscious effort to ignore her, to the point where I could no longer see her or hear her.

My mother didn't realize that she was shutting down my abilities to communicate with spirits. It would take decades for me to open up to those abilities again.

Pulling Away from the Spirit World

As infants, initially we don't see a difference between spirits and incarnate people. The soothing voice and smile of our spirit guide or a spirit animal or that of a loving, deceased relative comforts us and encourages us to continue our efforts to survive. Indeed, many of us have witnessed that as we rush to an infant who is screaming, we see the infant randomly smile and be comforted in their crib before we even get near them. While spirit guides and spirit animals may be helpful in calming infants, gradually the infant learns that spirits can't feed them. That is when incarnate people take precedence over spirits and the infant begins to ignore the spirits around them. After all, comfort/survival is all that really counts for an infant. Communicating with spirits is frosting. The Soul itself is part of the infant so their communication is by internal "knowing."

As mentioned, the Soul of the baby develops a kind of communication with the baby, which it continues to pursue as the baby grows up. As the baby detaches from spirits generally, as I did from Marilyn, she will also try to detach from her Soul and rely more on her Internal Rule Book for advice. Of course, there is never complete detachment from the Soul, but the communication between the Soul and its physical incarnation can vary tremendously from one child to the next. Good Soul/human communication usually translates as a child being very caring toward his peer group, while a child who is more detached from her Soul will be more aggressive and less compassionate in general.

This is not the child's fault. There are many factors that can create an angry child. What is important to note is that survival for that child is so difficult that the child doesn't pay attention to their Soul. An example would be a boy with an older brother who is very jealous of the attention his little brother gets and tries to bully him whenever he can get away with it.

Typically, as a child matures, it increasingly becomes a "material" girl or boy. For those children who have managed to open up to spiritual communication and have been allowed or even encouraged to pursue it, puberty and the pressures of adolescence usually snuff out any interest in continuing to communicate with spirits as time goes on. For a teenager struggling to adjust to a changing body and communicate with other teens, there just isn't any real interest in adding on some other kind of communication that's not universally accepted. Tammy is a good example of this.

Tammy's Tale

When Tammy was ten years old I helped her find a totem animal to be her spirit guide. This was a monkey she named Lacey. One day a friend of mine was visiting from another state. I decided to show the local, newly opened mall to my friend before taking her to the airport to catch her flight home. Tammy and her mom came with us. We spent too much time at the mall and got stuck in rush hour traffic on our way to the airport. It really looked like my friend would miss her flight. Tammy, sitting in the back seat behind me, leaned forward and whispered in my ear, "It's okay. I know we won't be late because Lacey told me that we'll get there on time." And she was right. We got there in plenty of time.

During adolescence, however, Tammy stopped communicating with Lacey as she filled all the hours of the day and night with conversations with her physical friends.

Who's the Boss?

As we've learned, initially there is a dance between the physical body dictating what is important to it—food and protection, security and reproduction—and the Soul trying to adapt to this physical body and orient it toward achieving the spiritual goals that were established prior to the individual's incarnation. This drive to achieve these spiritual goals may be very opaque and can manifest into inclinations or impulses we may have. For "some reason" we are drawn to a particular person or place, or we may be fascinated by a specific course of study or have a certain talent we're interested in exploring. This, in fact, is our Soul making suggestions as to the direction it would have us go.

Can You Hear Me?

The quality of the communication between a human body and its Soul makes a huge difference too. There is no obvious rule as to how this works; however, it's possible for a perfectly strong and able body to have a terrible connection with its Soul, while a physically challenged body may have a strong connection. Stephen Hawking is a good example of someone who had a physically challenged body but had a very strong connection to his Soul.

It's interesting to note that often when there is such a strong connection between the Soul and its human body, the human body can show extraordinary strength and resistance. This is part of the dance that exists between the Soul and the human body that it's trying to influence. The media occasionally report on people who embark on amazing acts of heroism: A soldier throws his body over a hand grenade to save the lives of his fellow soldiers. A fireman runs into a flaming building in an attempt to save the people and animals inside. A woman jumps onto a subway track to save a stranger who has fallen onto it.

These are all examples of a clear connection between the Soul and its human body. In each case the simple animal body would only save itself, but when coupled with the power of the Soul, again, amazing things can happen. This kind of connection can generate extraordinary physical strength, which is called "hysterical strength."

The true story of a woman who was able to lift a car single-handedly to save her child is a telling example. Imagine this mother, Angela Cavallo, watching a car slip off its jack and fall on her adult son Tony as he was underneath repairing it. Angela wasted no time lifting the car to free her son. This happened in 1982, in Lawrenceville, Georgia. Here Angela relied on the power of her physical body—her animal nature—coupled with her Soul to save her son. I'm sure she had additional help from other spirit guides around them.

Addiction

The human body has a highly developed mind where the Internal Rule Book stores everything that happens to that physical body. Based on that collection of data, a person makes decisions with the simple goals of survival, comfort, and love. The Soul tries to influence the human mind, but this can be a very difficult task. It is important to note that most of our decisions are done on autopilot. It often feels safer to us to replay what happened yesterday just because we survived it instead of living today. Decision-making is so tiring and, at times, risky for us humans that we like to create habits. Because it's so comfortable to create these habits, we create them throughout our day. We get accustomed to thinking of something else while we follow our routine. That is to say, we go on "automatic pilot," and when this happens we stop actively examining the initial decision that set it up. Meanwhile our Soul struggles to break us free from these habits, which is why we question our habits and consider changing them.

It is the body's mind under the influence of its Internal Rule Book that has trouble breaking habits. That is why it's important to periodically identify and review our routines and habits. Very often we are not even aware that we have fallen into any routine. While identifying and reviewing our routines, our Soul can inject some necessary changes as well as incorporate the qualities of kindness and compassion into all of our decisions.

The insidious way that any routine/habit is formed indicates the ease with which an addiction may arise. Innately we are all seeking a more comfortable life. The decision that seems to work to that end—like having a strong cup of coffee in the morning, for instance—can easily turn into an addiction. The coffee that makes us feel so good can help us again after lunch and then perhaps again after dinner to help us finish up some work.

Pretty soon one cup in the morning doesn't do it anymore, so we figure let's try two. Then we continue adding to that throughout the day. Before we know it, without our morning coffee we are a fire-breathing dragon. Our Soul can suggest we slow down but our body says, *I'm looking for comfort*. Once the body finds comfort in something, it is extremely hard for the Soul to be heard. Generally, the Soul and spirit guide work behind the scenes to involve the Souls of other people to help the addicted person break their habit.

Alcohol or drug addiction is obviously not so simple. Usually there are underlying reasons that seduce a person to initiate the use of an addictive substance. This can include self-medication when dealing with personal trauma. Once that substance gets into the physical body, it creates a desperate need for more. Some research shows that certain drugs can alter the brain to render it less able to make decisions, thereby making it harder to break an addiction. According to the National Institute on Drug Abuse website:

Drugs interfere with the way neurons send, receive, and process signals via neurotransmitters. Some drugs, such as marijuana and heroin, can activate neurons because their chemical structure mimics that of a natural neurotransmitter in the body. This allows the drugs to attach onto and activate the neurons. Although these drugs mimic the brain's own chemicals, they don't activate neurons in the same way as a natural neurotransmitter, and they lead to abnormal messages being sent through the network.

Other drugs, such as amphetamine or cocaine, can cause the neurons to release abnormally large amounts of natural neurotransmitters or prevent the normal recycling of these brain chemicals by interfering with transporters. This too amplifies or disrupts the normal communication between neurons.

The changed chemistry of the brain makes it more difficult for the Soul to communicate with the brain. Nevertheless, the Soul always has the potential of helping to reset the brain chemistry and facilitate a complete stop to any addiction.

How Spirits Help Break a Habit and an Addiction

Remember that the human body loves to develop routines and habits and is always seeking comfort, sometimes at any cost. The unchanging nature of routine/habit makes us feel safe because we fear change. It doesn't take long before we realize that even if we try to maintain the same routine, factors beyond our control can change things. We also might have some horrible entries in our Internal Rule Book that we can't forget as our Chatter Mind (more about this in chapter 3) taunts us with them. That coupled with the altering effects of drugs on our brain cells makes it tremendously difficult to break a drug or alcohol addiction. The Soul will try to pull someone out of the spiraling descent into addiction, but a strong physical support system is equally important. It is a group effort of spirits and physical people that can and do unite to save someone. Anyone can beat their addiction and remain drug or alcohol free.

ᴄᴈ How to Change a Routine or Break a Habit

This is a good exercise to change a routine or break a habit.

1. Observe your movements and thoughts. It's important to do this as an impartial observer with no value judgments. You might even jot down what you did. Are any of your actions or thoughts the same as yesterday and the day before that? Are you happy about these routines you have established? Then identify the routine or habit that you want to change. Your Soul can help you do this.

2. Once you have identified the routine you want to change, meditate and ask spirit why you need the routine. It brings you comfort, but why? And why do you need that comfort? Remember, no value judgments.

3. Find a way to reward yourself for each change in routine you make, even if it's only incremental. The key is to stay positive and upbeat. Your Soul and spirit guides will be your cheerleaders helping you to the finish line.

It might take several times to get rid of your routine permanently. Each return to the routine shouldn't be considered a failure but rather a step on a wiggly path toward your goal whereby you stay with the idea of forward motion instead of giving up. Soon you'll notice that the Universe is helping you by preventing you from getting what you need to maintain your routine or habit.

Alice's Habit

Alice loved her Starbucks venti matcha green tea latte. Every morning she ordered it ahead of time and loved picking it up as she walked her dog. Besides being a bit expensive for Alice, this wasn't too bad a habit, until Alice began searching for Starbucks when traveling. Alice was really miserable when she couldn't get her beverage in the morning. She realized that this had become a minor addiction.

As Alice meditated on where and how this all got started, she remembered being with her family in Denver, Colorado, at a mall. She *had asked a family member to buy her some green tea. The result was her first matcha green tea latte. She loved it. Her Internal Rule Book added this beverage as a plus, including the emotion of love since a loving family member had bought it for her. At home, Alice ordered this beverage because she liked it, but her Internal Rule Book associated the emotion of love with it.*

In other words, every time Alice had a Starbucks venti green tea latte she received a virtual hug. As she became a regular customer at her local Starbucks, the staff would greet her warmly, which reinforced the love component. When Alice understood the addictive nature of her routine, she began to step away from her daily drink. She also called in spirits and the Universe to help her. Suddenly that Starbucks always seemed to be out of matcha tea. Soon it became too much of a struggle to get her favorite beverage, and the routine ended. This may seem very simple, but the steps are the same for dealing with any habit.

First identify what makes the habit attractive. This will include emotional attachments that are guided by our Internal Rule Book. Separating all the emotional attachments dilutes their power and allows us to overcome each of them. When struggling to detach, personal energy and willpower are built up. Finally, the Universe will step in with help in various forms.

Our Animal Nature

To understand how our Soul operates in our lives we must have a proper understanding of the body of a human being. The physical body in which the Soul will reside for the life of that body is really just like that of any other mammal. Think in terms of a dog or a cat. As we know, initially the puppy or kitten has tremendous needs to be nurtured and cared for, but as it grows, its physical body increasingly becomes more independent, focusing on its physical needs.

Humans are quite similar. We are mammals with those same basic instincts to survive, reproduce, and seek pleasure. We grow up and to varying degrees we can be socialized and, dare I say, domesticated. In the well-known book *Lord of the Flies*, young boys by accident find themselves isolated from society at large. Left to their own devices, they create a violent and cruel society of survival of the fittest. Author William Golding believed it was the nature of man to create such a society.

It's a bit similar for a fetus. Even within her mother, the fetus absorbs all the nutrients she can get from the mother—even to the detriment of the mother. Again, it's all about survival. Without a Soul, humans would be more barbaric in nature than we already are. In fact, the overriding purpose of our Soul is to civilize our innate brute desire to survive at all costs. To a person, survival means accumulating as much as they can. With this comes the desire to control others and the environment. This applies not only to all of mankind in the collective but also to the actions and attitudes of individuals.

Learning to Walk the High Road

Down through time Souls have been working with mankind to develop a more socially minded human being. With this has come the development of our mental capacities to make choices that are based not simply on personal comfort and greed but actually take into account the welfare of others and our environment. The rules developed in our society—those governing fairness, respect, and, yes, love—are the result of the collective hard work of the Souls of innumerable people working to influence their animal nature so that we may all realize that the world can be heaven on Earth.

Looking at human development from the caveman to the twenty-first-century individual, it seems progress on this has been slow but steady. As we know, the basis of the progress is the search for comfort, which eventually includes the need for domination and control. Spiritual leaders such as Jesus, Mohammed, Moses, Buddha, and many others have lifted the bar of personal comfort to include kindness and mercy to others. They have introduced, on a large scale, the existence of the spirit world and the importance of demonstrating love and compassion in everyday life.

The Physical Body Brings in Baggage Too

As an individual matures, all too often its Soul has a hard time managing the physical impulses of its associated human body. Unfortunately, we are not all developing at the same speed, and regardless of how many times our Soul has incarnated, we are still challenged by the physical baggage of the body we incarnate into as well as our Soul's spiritual baggage. And all of this baggage complicates the ability of our Soul to communicate with our human body.

You might wonder how a physical body that decomposes and turns to dust can carry baggage from a past life into a new incarnation. The dust mixes with other dust and eventually it turns into a plant, a bug, an animal, or a new human being. How can all those random cells carry anything coherent? The magic is the DNA of the parents who conceive the new human being. It's through the parents' DNA that not only the memory of past-life events but also the thoughts and emotions attached to those events as they transpired are transferred. Whatever trauma was experienced in the past is captured in our cellular memory, that is, in our physical body/DNA. That's why simply identifying the source of a trauma and trying to deal with it intellectually doesn't work. We need to cleanse the cellular memory. For my clients I use Journey Work coupled with cleansing energy to do this, which is quite effective.

We witness these cellular memories occurring when young children display unusual reactions to things or events with which they have no prior experience. For example, a child might be terrified of a beautiful sweet cat for seemingly no reason. It's possible that in a past life that child had a traumatic encounter with a caracal or an Iberian lynx. Unfortunately rather than identify these reactions as part of the child's past-life baggage, we are more likely to explain it as some age-related developmental reaction.

Even though we like to think of a new life as a blank canvas, it's riddled with three-dimensional forms, squiggles, colors, etc. These come from the physical body baggage, Soul baggage, and scheduled events for the present incarnation. Add to that the general animal nature of a physical body and we can understand why we can feel so confused sometimes. The Soul tries to influence and guide its human body, but it is through our free will and choices that we create our life canvas. There is no previously set final image. Our human mind can decide what to pay attention to and what we allow to influence our lives. Beyond the initial markings on the canvas, our human mind paints the rest.

Because we have free will, all too often we manage to ignore the influence of our Soul and seek personal comfort/control instead, all the while stumbling over baggage obstacles brought in by both sides. In this, we may get ourselves into real trouble, believing that we know what we are doing to the point of not listening to any recommendations from our Soul, regardless of how much we could benefit from following them.

The Gall of It All

Clare's family had a history of gallbladder problems. Her grandfather, father, and brothers had all suffered from gallbladder disease, which caused problems in different ways and which required surgery. Clare was beginning to suffer from gallbladder problems too, and her doctor recommended surgery. Clare didn't like the idea so she went to see various healers in search of a different option.

The gallbladder represents anger and resentment. The healer she saw discovered that 128 years in the past, an event had transpired that had created the first gallbladder problem in Clare's bloodline, or DNA. With me, Clare researched what had initiated that precipitating event. She uncovered the horrendous story of one of her ancestors, who had mistreated people abominably. This male ancestor was full of anger and bitterness, which all too often he took out on others. In his debauched and cruel actions, he had initiated the gallbladder defect. Using this information, Clare and I freed her from that cellular memory (DNA connection) of that past life. We also had to clean up her dis-ease, that is the environmental factors in her current life that were making her feel angry and bitter. Her need for surgery vanished.

Shaping the Clay of the Newborn Self

For the most part when people look at a newborn baby, they believe that they're looking at wondrous clay. There is a basic shape to the clay but the infant seems so helpless and void of any personal power that it appears to be an empty vessel. However, as mentioned earlier, the physical body is composed, in part, of the DNA of its parents. This means that there is a certain amount of cellular memory that gets passed into a newborn child from the get-go. The parents themselves are chosen for an incarnation because of the cellular memories they will provide their fetus via their DNA. This includes physical frailties and other such problems, which can appear in the child's infancy or later on in life. This connection can also bring positive attributes such as muscular strength, a brilliant mind, or lots of energy.

Here a discussion of nature versus nurture is germane. What influences a person more, their environment or the hereditary physical abilities that show up as they mature? Does a child become a great athlete because of personal mentoring or because they have physical agility in their DNA? Does a child become a great scientist because of their education or is it thanks to their lineage, which holds a number of scientific geniuses?

Most people ignore the possibility that this darling, fragile miracle of life that we see as a baby has a long history of cellular memories from its parents' incarnations—good and bad—which carries into the present life. This may include a propensity for certain beliefs and reactions to stimuli. Some babies will howl until their needs are met. Others will simply tolerate the discomfort until someone is ready to tend to them. This is a product of their unique physical cellular memory.

A Reluctant Fetus

Because of the physical nature of animal life where survival reigns supreme, sometimes a fetus isn't strong enough to make it. In this case the mother's body will respond by ending the pregnancy in a miscarriage.

Babies who are born prematurely and who probably would have died only a few years ago, can now survive. Baby Saybie, considered to be the world's smallest baby, weighed 8.6 ounces when she was born at twenty-three weeks in December of 2018 in San Diego and—she survived! This is an example of how we're able to tame the forces of nature, which would otherwise excise the weak and the fragile.

On the other hand our Soul can influence a woman to have an abortion to postpone an incarnation for a variety of reasons. The fetus is always part of this decision-making and agrees to the postponement of its incarnation. The result is the creation of a healthier society where an incarnation can happen under the best circumstances.

Throughout our lives this struggle between the Soul and the natural inclinations of a human continues. What our human self naturally can do and what our Soul inspires it to do—not only physically, but also mentally and spiritually—is always evolving. And as we continue to evolve as human beings with a Soul, we begin to experience this thing called love.

About Love

It's important to note that no emotions exist in the spirit world and thus our Soul and other helping spirits don't experience love. That means the Soul can only experience passionate love through their incarnated human. This is the same for helper spirit guides. Love as we know it is carnal pleasure, like eating and sex. It is one of the body's perks, to experience emotions, good and bad.

One of the milestones we reach in our development as human beings is when we begin to experience love. However, at this time we also begin to believe that love is conditional. This begins as a transactional relationship between a person feeding an infant and the infant itself. At this stage the infant might think, *I feel good when someone feeds me, but I can't trust everyone to feed me. Some people do and some people don't. I like the people who feed me. I don't care so much for those who don't.* Or *I like that person who makes noises and funny faces.* This is also transactional: *You make me laugh, so I like you. You provide me with comfort, and I'll do the smile thing for you.*

Although pure love is unconditional, the idea that love is conditional continues to develop. This is a complicated idea right from the start and becomes increasingly more so as we get older and define love more harshly. Our Internal Rule Book is constantly creating expectations and recording disappointments. Hurt gets mixed into love, and love is no longer always so nice. We experience rejection. We learn to be careful of how we express love and also how to be skeptical of those trying to love us. At the same time our capacity to love is often limited to fewer and fewer people. Trust becomes a real issue. First love is so sweet because it's so honest.

Into the confusion of love comes simple chemistry; we are mysteriously attracted to some people and not others. Initially we are attracted to those people who are physically related to us. It's almost as though the sensitivity to those vital people around us at birth later, as we grow up, transforms into a sensitivity of potential love with a capital *L*. Physical and spiritual past-life baggage influences our choice making too. This causes all kinds of celebration and drama.

A Baby as Pure Love

Regardless of the manner of conception, a baby is an example of pure love. Even though some babies may be conceived as a result of a horrendous and violent act, that individual's potential to give and receive unconditional love remains strong. As discussed in the previous section, that unconditional love soon becomes confused when the developing child begins to define love as transactional. As the infant turns into a toddler and grows up, any and all *nurture* (vs. *nature*) experiences can be full of love or completely devoid of it.

When interacting with clients, I often use Journey Work to reconnect them with the unconditional love that they came into life with, which again has nothing to do with their physical conception. This helps them to break through the accumulated baggage that prevents them from feeling love and/or being able to love.

Vinnie's Story

Vinnie was in his late forties when he came to see me. He was tall and muscular and would have been good-looking if he hadn't had such a menacing demeanor. He looked like a dangerous thug. When addressed, his voice sounded like an angry, scary bark. I could feel that Vinnie had a good heart and needed healing. His parents had had a terrible marriage and finally divorced. His abusive father left, taking Vinnie's brother with him. Vinnie preferred to stay with his mother although she really couldn't take care of him. Left to his own devices Vinnie spent his youth getting in trouble. He married too young and had two sons. He was a terrible husband and father and finally abandoned his wife and kids.

Vinnie turned to drugs and alcohol. After repeated warnings he ended up in prison for driving under the influence, or DUI. That was an eye-opener for him. He sobered up and tried to pull his life together and catch up on his child support payments by working construction. Just when he felt he was on the right track, one of his sons, the one who would actually still talk to him, got leukemia and died. Vinnie quit construction and got a job as a bouncer in a club. He enjoyed beating people up.

Vinnie's problem was that he had completely disengaged from the intrinsic love within him. As I connected him to the truly loving person he was, he quit his job as a bouncer. He said he didn't like beating people up anymore. As he continued to open up he connected with his son who had passed. This brought great comfort to Vinnie. Gradually he began studying Reiki and became a Reiki practitioner. Once Vinnie could tap into the love that the universe offers to all of us, he became a very good healer, helping others to feel the love as well.

3

The Internal Rule Book and the Chatter Mind

EVERYTHING IN OUR PHYSICAL LIFE is recorded in our subconscious mind as a rule in what I call our Internal Rule Book, which I first introduced to you in chapter 1. Why do I call it a rule book instead of a ledger? Because whatever is in it rules our life. We have no control over what is recorded. It's automatic and begins when we're a fetus, and we become aware of the sounds around us and very much in touch with the emotions experienced by our mother.

When I was pregnant, I played a compilation of my favorite classical music over and over again. When my daughter was born, all I had to do was play that compilation, and she would be comforted. Her Internal Rule Book triggered joy and memories of being nurtured and protected.

Again, everything we hear, feel, or experience is automatically recorded in our subconscious mind as we experience life—and for each recording there is a value judgment added. This creates rules that bring us joy as well as fear and anxiety. Originally this was done to protect our animal body. If a fetus heard loud voices arguing, such as when Mom and Dad were having a fight, the equation would be loud voices equal danger. If a fetus heard loud voices laughing, like those of the children playing next door, the equation would be loud voices equal fun. Those equation entries became rules that we would then automatically follow.

All of our future physical and emotional reactions are influenced by what we experienced in the past, how we perceived those events, and whether they were considered positive or negative, safe or dangerous.

For our survival, emotions were hardwired to our Internal Rule Book as an immediate response mechanism. We didn't need to think about what to do; our emotions dictated our physical reaction. The result is that we immediately react to a stimulus before we're able to consciously evaluate what's going on.

By the time we are a year old our Internal Rule Book is already functioning well. We are very opinionated about the people we like and those we don't. The more systematically and tenderly someone satisfies our needs, the more likely we are to love that person. Following the guidance of our Internal Rule Book we also learn what we can do to keep ourselves safe and loved. If Mom gets angry at us we might think she won't take care of us anymore. We take note of what pleases her and what makes her unhappy, and we often incorporate this into erroneous beliefs about ourselves.

The Internal Rule Book in Action

Our Internal Rule Book always controls our emotions and completely bypasses our logical mind altogether. When an event occurs, our Internal Rule Book attaches an emotion to it. This means that in our daily life, before we know it, we are happy, sad, distressed, or irritated. Suddenly our heart is thumping happily, or we are furious. Or perhaps we are completely depressed. It takes our mind a while to catch up, but by the time it does we're saturated with an emotion and often "we just can't think straight." This is because our thoughts are filtered through our emotions, which are generated by our Internal Rule Book.

As a result, we may wind up with the completely wrong analysis of an event and then suffer the wrong emotion. For instance, so often children feel at fault when their parents argue or divorce. Even the tragedy of a child believing that the sexual abuse they were subjected to was their own fault gets written into their Internal Rule Book and reflects back to them their belief that they're not a good person

Sarah's Negative Body Image

Sarah was eleven years old, and her body was beginning to change given that she was entering puberty. In class the teacher wanted the students to experience the benefits of standing up straight and breathing deeply. Sarah, who was tall for her age and had a tendency to slouch because of her height, breathed in deeply and pulled her shoulders back. She felt great! That is, until her classmate Judy pointed at her and began to laugh. Judy was pointing at Sarah's budding breasts, which were slightly visible under her sweater. Sarah was mortified. She hated her body, and she crumpled herself back into a slouch. At that moment a rule was written in Sarah's Internal Rule Book: my body is ugly. Sarah never would have intentionally created a rule like that about herself, but it was written and would stay with her until she was able to change it.

Once a rule is in our rule book we unwittingly continue to reinforce it. For example, eleven-year-old Sarah, as an adult, will have trouble accepting compliments about her physical body. She will be much more likely to ignore those compliments and accept negative comments instead.

A Mother's Influence

Veronica's mother had a bizarre love/hate relationship with her daughter. It seemed like she projected her own lack of self-esteem onto Veronica by constantly berating her for everything. Veronica learned to be quiet and never confront her mother. To Veronica, staying under-cover was the only safe place to be.

As a child, whenever she was in a social situation with her mother, inevitably her mother would at some point grab Veronica's forearm and plunge her sharp fingernails into her arm. This was a signal that Veronica was doing or saying something wrong. If someone complimented

Veronica, the mother would give a resigned sigh, indicating that she knew the compliment wasn't real. Veronica was often told how unappealing she was and how disagreeable and poorly behaved to boot. All these events were recorded in Veronica's Internal Rule Book as follows:

Avoid social situations because they can lead to personal pain or later punishment.

Don't bother trying to look nice.

You are simply an ugly brute.

Robert's Critical Teacher

Robert was in the third grade. One day his math teacher took him aside and explained to him that some people were good in math and some were not. The teacher elaborately continued to point out how Robert was not good in math and never would be. Needless to say Robert's Internal Rule Book included the following beliefs:

Stop trying to learn math. You are not capable of doing better.

Stop trying to do well in school. You are not smart.

Fireflies

It was Jennifer's birthday. She was turning four. Her party, attended by her own friends and also the friends of her parents, lasted into the night. It was so exciting and glorious that when some fireflies magically appeared, Jennifer believed them to be the crowning event of her special day. From that day on, throughout her life, every time Jennifer saw a firefly, she would feel overwhelming joy.

Beth, also four years old, was at home alone. Her parents had gone to the big city to go shopping. Her older brother was supposed to be with her, but he was out with his friends. Nighttime came and Beth began to feel hungry and afraid. She decided to go out and look for her brother. She opened the door and a firefly flew into her face. Beth screamed and slammed the door. She ran to her room and hid until her parents finally came home. After that incident every time Beth saw a firefly she shuddered.

Pipe Down!

Susie was two years old and had just found her voice as a singer. She was excited and ran to her mother to share her discovery.

"Mommy, Mommy!" she yelled out as she began to sing at the top of her voice.

"Susie, stop! Please! Not so loud! Not now!" her mother said. She was suffering from a horrendous migraine and couldn't stand any loud sounds. "Mommy doesn't feel well."

Susie was crushed and stopped singing. A belief was added to her Internal Rule Book: my singing makes people sick. With that also came a new look at love. Maybe Mommy doesn't love me all the time, she might wonder. Accompanied by this was the belief that Mommy wasn't a reliable source of nurture.

Alice Is Trapped by Her Past

Alice and her husband, Greg, were arguing, and as the fight intensified Greg continued to raise his voice. Soon Greg's booming voice seemed to fill the room in a menacing way. Alice felt as though she was captured in a giant bell that was making a deafening noise. She felt trapped and powerless. Defeated, she left the room in tears, allowing Greg to once again have his way. This happened every time she and Greg had an argument. Alice hated feeling so trapped and powerless. She felt inferior to Greg and believed his opinion mattered more than hers.

What Alice didn't realize was that when Greg raised his voice Alice automatically turned into a frightened and powerless little girl. It turned out that the origin of this behavior was Alice's father. When she was very young, between the ages of three and eight, her father physically beat up her mother. That savagery always began with an argument that got louder and louder until finally her father's voice boomed over the sounds of him hitting her mother and her mother's painful cries. Alice had learned to avoid a loud argument at all costs because she believed it would lead to physical pain.

Alice didn't remember any of this as Greg yelled at her, but her

Internal Rule Book in her subconscious mind did, and it triggered her reactions of fear and defeat. When Alice experienced the trauma of her parents' physical fight, a rule to be followed in the future was created, joining the many others in her Internal Rule Book. So when Greg shouted at her, she would cower from him to physically protect herself even though he was not going to hurt her physically.

All of us have automatic reactions to different stimuli. Through trial and error our bodies let us know to be careful with fire or stay away from certain foods that have made us sick in the past. All this information about what works for us physically is written in our personal Internal Rule Book. We don't need to get burned again to remember that fire is hot and that we should be careful around it. In the same vein, once we've identified something that's made us sick, we'll automatically avoid it in future. We go on automatic pilot and allow our bodies to navigate according to the rules tucked away in our Internal Rule Book.

Because our emotions are triggered by our Internal Rule Book in the same way that our physical reactions are, Alice not only automatically withdrew to protect herself, she felt frightened. She wasn't really afraid of Greg; it was his booming voice yelling at her that triggered her childhood memories of her father beating up her mother. As a result, Alice automatically became afraid of Greg whenever they had a fight.

Mitigating the Internal Rule Book

As we saw in Alice's story, when a particular rule in our Internal Rule book is triggered, we can experience an immediate fight-or-flight reaction, but it's good to remember that reaction can be mitigated with wisdom.

The first trick is to overcome the rules in our personal Internal Rule Book by identifying the beliefs stored there. However, because these beliefs activate our emotions automatically, it's pretty darn hard to overcome them. And it isn't a lot of fun to delve into traumatic events. In the story above, Alice was consumed by feelings of fear and impotence, which demanded concession to her aggressor. It wasn't easy to surmount these emotions, but as I worked with Alice, once she could recognize her predisposed reaction dictated by her Internal Rule Book, she could begin to stay in the present and see herself as a strong adult who could not only defend herself but could also refuse to be bullied. With the addition of energy healing to cleanse her of the cellular memory of her trauma, Alice became very bold and strong.

Bernadette Wants to Get Pregnant

Bernadette's mother came to me in distress because Bernadette had problems conceiving. She had been married for three years and still there was no sign of a baby. According to her mother, Bernadette was upset by her barren status. Apparently the medical community couldn't find any reason for her lack of fertility.

When Bernadette came to my office, professing that she wanted a child badly and that she was heartbroken because she'd not been able to conceive, I proceeded to conduct a journey with her. She lay down and I gave her some energy to pump up her vibration. I did this by putting my hands on or near her head and then channeling energy through her entire nervous system. It had a very calming and fulfilling effect. Bernadette began the Journey Work to find out what was preventing her from getting pregnant.

Dipping into her childhood spontaneously, Bernadette brought up a memory of her family's struggles. She was an only child growing up and, as such, was surrounded by adults. One day she overheard her parents having an argument. This was unusual as they seemed to always get along. They were arguing about how to manage their difficult financial situation. They wanted to travel but couldn't afford it. In their fight they articulated that Bernadette was a heavy financial burden for them and wondered how they would ever manage.

Overhearing this, Bernadette internalized the message that children could be a terrible burden to a loving couple and that, more spe-cifically, children could prevent their parents from traveling and living life fully! Bernadette's Internal Rule Book had immediately registered this rule.

Bernadette was very much in love with her husband, and they loved to take long trips together. Her deep-seated, heretofore hidden belief was that a child would ruin her relationship with her husband, who didn't seem to particularly want a child anyway.

Even after revealing this hidden information Bernadette still insisted that she wanted a baby. I asked her who would take care of the child if she had one. She hesitated and then said, "My mother." In other words, it was really Bernadette's mother who wanted a grandchild.

I explained to Bernadette that having a baby would not be the end of her happy life as part of a married couple. She should wait a bit, perhaps even a few years, without worrying about getting pregnant. After that she would conceive in joy. And she did!

Who Put That L on Your Forehead?

I used to work as a TV producer, and at one point it seemed as though none of my projects were coming to fruition. So I decided that the proj-ect I was working on at the time would be my final effort. If I didn't succeed with this particular project, I would be a complete failure.

After a great deal of effort I eventually found a funder for the proj-ect. I was elated! To highlight how important this funder was to me, I invited him to lunch to discuss our deal.

On the day of our lunch meeting I was on top of the world. Everything was falling into place nicely! As a courtesy I called my funder to confirm our lunch. He told me that he was too busy to have lunch that day. "No problem," I answered sweetly. "I'll just send over the paperwork regarding your funding. You'll just need to approve it."

"Oh, yes, about that. It's not going to work out after all," he said.

With those words my heart sank, and I began to feel like the ultimate Loser. This was it. I had blown it. My project was dead. I was *dead. As though I didn't feel bad enough my Chatter Mind (see the following section) jumped in and told me that had I not called earlier to confirm our lunch, he would have stood me up. I became deeply depressed.*

Fortunately I had made plans to visit my friend Rosalee in Manhattan prior to meeting the funder for lunch. When I arrived at Rosalee's apartment and explained what had happened, she was wonderful! She sympathized with me about the sad outcome I had just experienced, but to my surprise, she kept reiterating how happy she was to see me. She was especially happy that we could now have lunch.

I was confused. Didn't she see the giant L for Loser written across my forehead?

I began reflecting on why Rosalee didn't see the L and didn't consider me a loser. If she hadn't seen the L, who had? With horror I realized that I was the one who saw myself as a Loser. I was the one who had created the rule, "If I don't succeed with this project I will be a complete Loser." Automatically this definition appeared in my Internal Rule Book.

Gradually I began to realize that I could choose to have different reactions to the loss of my funder. Who had identified this funder as the last possibility? Me. I had done that. I realized that if I created that rule, I could change it. Then, realizing that the source of all my emotions is my Internal Rule Book, I discovered how to access it and change the rules that it contained. Although the realization that I had set up that rule regarding my funder, my Internal Rule Book wouldn't let go of it so easily. I used deep meditation and energy work to completely release that rule.

The Chatter Mind

Connected to our Internal Rule Book is an automatic alert system that communicates with our conscious mind. It's a separate voice that keeps random thoughts running continuously through our head. I call that voice our "Chatter Mind" because it incessantly comments on everything.

The Chatter Mind is the voice of our Internal Rule Book and as we know, the Internal Rule Book puts a value judgment on everything that happens to us. We wake up in the morning and immediately our Chatter Mind begins reminding us of the rules that correspond with what's going on. Have we woken up too early or too late? This is usually followed by either kudos for getting up at the right time or more often than not, berating ourselves for staying in bed too long or even getting up too early and thus not getting enough sleep. We contemplate our agenda for the day, and the Chatter Mind jumps in with opinions about all of it.

This could be followed by unpleasant remarks about how we aren't doing our job very well because we are too disorganized or not smart enough or some other negative belief. The Chatter Mind seems to have something to say about everything! It also can take any event or conversation and embroider it into a whole story. That story can be pleasant or it can be extremely upsetting.

Originally the Chatter Mind was, like the Internal Rule Book, a useful tool that helped us to survive. For example, if we were taught to wait for the light to turn red for cars and green for pedestrians, we will always have a hard time crossing a street against the light because our Internal Rule Book will command our Chatter Mind to remind us we are breaking a dangerous rule. In this case, our Chatter Mind is our friend. However, all too often our Chatter Mind is not our friend. We humans tend to be very creative thinkers. We get started on a topic and then we like to figure it out by considering it from a variety of angles. This is where our Internal Rule Book and Chatter Mind come in. Together they embellish a story and, before you know it, an unlikely scenario has been created.

For example, you might remember having a crush on someone in junior high or high school. One day this crush accidentally bumps into you in the hallway, knocking your books out of your arms. He catches your arm as you almost trip. He is truly sorry and apologizes, helping you pick up your books. You are flushed with pleasure and overwhelmed with love. As he walks away your Chatter Mind takes over: *He touched your arm. He must definitely like you. Did you notice how he looked into your eyes?* Depending on the level of your self-esteem, these Chatter Mind comments can also turn into, *What a stupid klutz you are! There he was and you didn't say anything clever! You didn't even tell him your name!*

As you can see, all of this turns into a sticky mess when emotions take over, which they do immediately. The intoxicating pleasure of your crush touching your arm can be dashed at the thought of him thinking you were a clumsy fool. Thanks to your Chatter Mind and Internal Rule Book, you might spend weeks in the flush of love or in the depths of despair—all based on an innocuous event.

The Chatter Mind Interferes

Sarah and Sam were driving in a car. They had been dating for a year and were soon to move in together. Sarah's Chatter Mind had been busy telling her how wonderful it would be to live with Sam and reminded Sarah that it was the first-year anniversary of their first date. Her Internal Rule Book and Chatter Mind had Sarah lost in dreamy bliss, imagining romance while living with her beloved Sam, who would always be the perfect man in her life. Full of expectations of his loving response—a smile, or perhaps a kiss—she looked lovingly at Sam and noted, "Today is the one-year anniversary of our first date." Reflecting on when he'd first met Sarah, Sam remembered that he had been on his way to get the recall adjustment on his car done but because he ran into Sarah he got sidetracked and it slipped his mind and never happened. With this, Sam realized that he had forgotten about it and still hadn't done the recall adjustment! He was horrified and angry at himself.

Sam's Internal Rule Book and Chatter Mind took over as he heard his father's voice lecturing him about how important manufacturer recalls were. Was there a window on having it done and was it now too late? Chatter Mind repeated his father's words that implied he was incompetent. Sam got a disturbed look on his face as he listened to his Chatter Mind. Sarah, meanwhile, had expected Sam to smile and say something sweet to her, but viewing the expression on his face, she now thought maybe he didn't really love her after all. Her Internal Rule Book and Chatter Mind reminded her of her previous boyfriend who had suddenly and unceremoniously dumped her.

"You're moving in with me next week!" Sarah said with an edge to her voice.

Sam, who was still thinking about when he could get the recall done, emerged from his thoughts and mumbled, "What?"

"What? You're asking 'What?' We talked about this for two months! It was your idea. You brought it up!" Sarah snarled.

"I did? I mean, I did. I did," Sam mumbled, still a bit lost in the conversation.

"So you did want to move in with me but now you don't want to anymore!" Sarah declared. "Well, I don't want you to move in with me, either!"

This conversation between Sarah and Sam is a perfect example of how our Internal Rule Book triggers our emotions and creates expectations. For Sarah, living with a man she loved was a wonderful adventure for her that filled her with passion, and she expected her boyfriend, Sam, to show the same emotions for her. Meanwhile Sam's Internal Rule Book had him reeling in concern and anger because he'd forgotten to service his car and worried about what his father would say if he found out. Sarah's emotions of love and passion and her expectation of a loving response from Sam collided with Sam's emotions of concern and anger and his feelings of incompetence. Clearly, they weren't on the same page—their individual Internal Rule Books had taken them to opposing places. Had they been stripped of the interfering Internal Rule Book and the Chatter Mind, they would have been fine.

Expectations

When our Internal Rule Book and Chatter Mind set up expectations, and those expectations aren't met, we're confused, hurt, sad, angry, and deeply wounded. Our expectations as to how anything will work out seem to happen automatically in our conscious mind. The expectations could present themselves as benchmarks to assess if a project will manifest or not. The Internal Rule Book carries the building blocks of the walls around us, preventing us from pursuing a project or giving and receiving love. Overriding those walls seems very risky but is an extremely rewarding reason to rewrite one's Internal Rule Book.

Dottie's Erroneous Assumptions

Dottie was in her seventies and enjoyed playing golf with her friends. It was always the high point of her week as well as a personal achievement because she'd created the original group. One day Dottie tripped on an icy street and injured her knee. After surgery and a year of rehab Dottie rejoined her golf group. She began slowly by playing as a substitute when someone couldn't make it. Dottie was currently taking golf lessons and wanted to return to the group full-time. The present group leader, Caroline, didn't extend an invitation to Dottie to join full-time, however. When Dottie confronted Caroline, Caroline tried to tell Dottie that she was better off remaining a substitute.

When I spoke with Dottie she had spent several days ruminating over her conversation with Caroline. At this point Dottie felt betrayed and inadequate. She was crushed and doubted her own golfing ability. Over and over in her mind she embroidered the story to include her mother's voice berating her for never being good enough and being a nuisance. Dottie coupled that with the idea that she held everyone up, that the other women didn't really like her, and that she could never be a good enough golfer despite having taken many golf lessons.

In Caroline's conversation with Dottie she had indeed said the things Dottie accused her of saying; however, they weren't meant to be hurtful. It wasn't that Caroline didn't like Dottie. It seemed that Caroline had simply decided to replace Dottie with a personal friend of hers, assuming that Dottie wouldn't be interested in participating as more than a substitute. Caroline had extended the invitation to her friend and felt she couldn't retract it now.

Meanwhile Dottie's Chatter Mind had created a miserable story for her; one that certainly wasn't based in the truth of the situation. We humans have the questionable talent of spinning false stories based on our Chatter Mind and our Internal Rule Book.

After a session with me, Dottie called Caroline and demanded her spot in the group. Caroline immediately agreed. Dottie was surprised at how quickly and easily Caroline acquiesced. After that, Dottie enjoyed playing golf with her friends again, even surprising them with her improvement in the game.

Meditation to the Rescue

Many people who are authorities on meditation tell us that we have access to all the answers we need via meditation. I believe this is true. How this works is that it is our Soul that can access all the information we could ever want. Given this, and the fact that meditation enhances our mind/Soul communication, just add some energy cleansing work and voila! We can alleviate the damage done by our Internal Rule Book and Chatter Mind.

It's true that being in meditation, away from the maddening crowd—either in our own quiet space or on a retreat in nature—is conducive to Soul communication because we're able to mitigate potential triggers that constantly spring from the stimuli around us. But although meditation can be a wonderful way to handle an emotional trigger and help you to silence the Chatter Mind, or at least muffle it a bit, it won't eliminate damage done by the Internal Rule Book unless you've already created the necessary internal rule that posits that meditation will bring you peace. In fact, if you try to impose meditation in the middle of an emotional tsunami, you could be making your situation more difficult for yourself. You might feel you aren't meditating correctly so instead of invoking peace and calm, you might be feeding the fire by adding another reason why you're a screwup: you can't even meditate right!

The best approach is to create a meditation process that you do when you're feeling good. If you set up your own sacred space and perhaps your own altar, you might add a special shawl you wear while meditating. Every time you meditate for even five minutes, try to use the shawl and the same meditation space. Picture the shawl as a protective blanket designed to instill a sense of hopeful tranquility.

The chaos that we experience and that requires our remediation is caused by a mind that's all too frequently clouded by emotion. While meditating at the right time and in the right frame of mind can certainly help, what we really need to do is create a paradigm where hope is the overriding factor. In that paradigm, anything is possible. A person can be on their deathbed and spontaneously recover. This is a definite possibility, albeit a rare one. It's all about picking yourself up, facing another day, adjusting expectations and desires, being grateful for what is, and finding things and people to love and identifying and accepting the love that is offered to you.

This requires us to constantly be aware of what's in our Internal Rule Book. For example, in the story of Sam and Sarah, if Sam had been aware of his thoughts he might have begun to wonder why he was thinking about his father's disapproval and stop allowing his thoughts to carry him to a very sad place. The same can be said for Sarah. Her Internal Rule Book triggered the painful memory of her ex-boyfriend and fear that Sam didn't care for her anymore. Awareness is the key.

The more we seek out happy and funny things to read, watch, or listen to, and the more we participate in enjoyable interactions with family and friends, the more we feed our Internal Rule Book's experiences of joy and positivity, which will serve us well in difficult times.

So although they are not always easy to do, the basic steps to overcoming the dictates of the Internal Rule Book and the Chatter Mind are as follows:

1. Be aware that your Internal Rule Book and its Chatter Mind exist and may be affecting you negatively.
2. Distance yourself from that Chatter Mind by understanding that it can be ignored.
3. Learn to temper all your emotions so that when an emotional tsunami arrives, it doesn't drown you.
4. Seek out enjoyable experiences and put a positive spin on all of life's events. In other words, always look for the silver lining!
5. Make a Happy Go-To List of five solo activities that you can use to distract yourself from spiraling into anger or depression. On my list I have soft serve vanilla ice cream that's dipped in chocolate that hardens. Going to a special place, watching a special show, or reading a funny book are all possibilities.

We will look at other ways to positively overcome the directives of the Internal Rule Book and the Chatter Mind in chapter 6.

4

How the Internal Rule Book Can Define Your Identity

IN ADDITION TO BEING A RULE BOOK that sets up the rules by which we conduct our lives, the Internal Rule Book forms our perception of who we are. Our experiences, reactions, emotions, and consequences are collected in our rule book. As discussed previously, without skipping a beat our Internal Rule Book records everything that happens to us and tries to make sense of it all. Inevitably, as we age, we're rewarded or held accountable for certain events. All of this gets recorded too. The result can add to our previously formed beliefs about ourselves, good or bad: I am pretty; I am smart; I am good; I am successful; I am bad; I am ugly; I am dumb; I am a failure. It doesn't take much for something damaging to find its way into our Internal Rule Book!

Let's look at one's view of success as an example. One person's idea of success could be another person's idea of failure. One man, Phil, might consider that working hard and bringing home lots of money for the family is success. Another man, Stan, might think that staying at home and working hard to raise his children while his wife works at a corporate job is success. Both can be fine with their personal definition of success *except when their Internal Rule Book muddies the water.*

Phil's Internal Rule Book is in line with his work at a corporation because it allows him to bring home lots of money; therefore Phil is happy. Stan, on the other hand, feels dissatisfied staying at home with the kids even though his wife and children are thriving, and he actually enjoys staying at home with his kids. His Chatter Mind, voicing his Internal Rule Book, however, tells him that only a failure sits at home with his children and allows his wife to support him. It's possible that this rule was written when his father described a stay-at-home dad as a lazy bum: "What kind of excuse for a man would have his wife work while he sat at home all day?" he would say. Occasionally Stan hears his father's words ringing in his ears even though the truth is that his family very much supports the division of responsibilities he has worked out with his wife.

This idea of "doing what I should be doing" gets further clouded when our Internal Rule Book gets filled with what people say while we're growing up. "You must be a lawyer. Everyone in the family is one except Uncle Herbie. He's a little strange." Or "This is a family of electricians. It's in your blood." Each of us has special talents, and we have to fight to overcome the mandates of our Internal Rule Book if, according to those mandates, our talents are considered inappropriate.

Because it's important to identify many of the ways the Internal Rule Book can hurt us, I've focused on that aspect of it here.

A Burden to the World

Monica always felt unworthy of being loved. Her list of failures included not being attractive or smart enough, being too heavy, clumsy, and awkward, and so on. She didn't find out until late in life that she had been conceived during semiconsensual intercourse that her mother had with a coworker and had spent her life trying to conceal from her husband. In the mix was Monica's paternal grandmother who saw through the ruse and never let anyone forget it. She tried to have Monica's parents abort her, which they almost did. Unfortunately, this same grandmother was called upon to babysit Monica when she was very young while both parents worked. This resulted in Monica almost dying from pneumonia when she was six months old.

Needless to say, Monica's Internal Rule Book was full of notes about being unwelcome for a variety of reasons. In addition, her three older brothers were wickedly cruel in reminding her of all of her negative traits in front of their mother, who would simply look sadly at Monica in complicit silence. Monica grew up believing she was a burden to the world.

When she was in fourth grade she fell ill with a blood disorder. Beverly, a girl she knew, had fallen ill with a similar illness a year earlier. Monica remembered seeing her at school; she was pale and looked extremely weak. Beverly died shortly after that. Fortunately, Monica was part of a wonderful church school program, and she developed a deep friendship with Jesus. That relationship provided the unconditional love that Monica needed to survive her illness. Additional healing came from an unlikely source: Monica's mother, who said that she wanted to help her heal because, as she told Monica, "The worst thing that can happen to a mother is to lose her child." Since Monica felt her mother didn't really appreciate her, she believed that it wasn't so much about Monica dying that bothered her mother; it was more that her mother didn't want to have to face the trauma of losing a child.

Throughout her life Monica never caught up with who she really was. She expected to be bullied and treated poorly. She rarely stood up for herself and basically floated through life, accepting the good things that occasionally did happen as anomalies. She constantly felt she was doing the wrong thing, and anyone who considered her a good person probably didn't know her very well. She felt she had an evil core and didn't have close friends because she was concerned they would discover this about her. Of course she did not have an evil core and with a considerable amount of self-help work and help from me, Monica eventually realized she was a very good person and that a world filled with Monicas wouldn't be so bad.

Regardless of these revelations and aha moments, Monica couldn't allow herself to feel good. There was always a voice criticizing her every move, accompanied by the sharp emotions of depression and fear. I worked with Monica to identify the source of her trauma, address it, and then clear out any and all attached cellular memories that were holding her back.

As Monica was able to question her emotions instead of losing herself in them, she began to control her Internal Rule Book. In fact, Monica went on to rewrite some of the rules in her rule book.

To understand ourselves better it's important to assess where we are in life. Figuring out what our present reality is will tell us the truth of our lives. For Monica, this means that today she can look at herself as the lovely, kind person she truly is, without bowing to a false set of rules dictated by her Internal Rule Book. Instead, she can live her essence, which she, like all of us, was born to do.

Patty's Skewed Self-Image

Our Internal Rule Book can cause us tremendous pain at any point in our life. Patty was the mother of six young children. Despite having to care for all of them, Patty always looked perfect. She also always had a quick smile and exuded sweetness. This gentleness hid a fierce warrior who was a remarkable defender of her own children and other children in the community as well. Needless to say, Patty quickly became popular and well known in the neighborhood. Although this caused some jealousy among the other moms, Patty walked to the beat of her own drum and didn't let that affect her. She also was the picture of health.

One day Patty began to experience excruciating back pain, which had no discernible cause. It was completely debilitating for her, and she ended up spending weeks in bed, which turned into months. She had all kinds of medical treatments for her back, but nothing seemed to help in any consistent way.

Patty did some Journey Work with me. Her father came up first.

Gradually Patty's story came out. When she was a child, her father used to randomly beat her because, according to him, she was bad. The beatings continued until one day Patty, then a teenager, ran away. When she finally returned home, her parents seemed to have been frightened enough by her disappearance that her father never beat her again. Patty nevertheless had a rule written that she was somehow a bad person.

In her adult life, even though her children were doing very well in school, and Patty was doing an excellent job as mother and wife to her loving husband, she believed she was somehow doing something wrong but, as with the beatings, she didn't know what that was. This terrified her to the point of withdrawing from everyday life and hiding in pain. She was punishing herself for no reason, and her back pain was the physical manifestation of that impulse to punish herself.

The way we changed that rule in her Internal Rule Book was for Patty to realize that she was doing a great job as a wife and mother and for her to acknowledge that, when she was young, her father had taken out his personal anger and frustration on her for no reason. Through Journey Work we rescued that abused little girl. As Patty changed the rule in her Internal Rule Book that said she was severely incompetent in ways that she couldn't identify herself, her back started improving. There was a direct relationship between her body and her Internal Rule Book.

The Wounded Child as a Product of the Internal Rule Book

Ginger was beautiful and fun and normally sweet, but she had unexpected flashes of anger that would bring out a sharp tongue. More than one person had been shocked and wounded by Ginger's comments. When Ginger and I worked together, we discovered that she was a wounded child. In Journey Work she remembered how, as a child, her mother would tell her that she'd always wanted a daughter and that when Ginger was born, she was joyful.

Ginger's mother already had two sons, and she finally had her long-awaited daughter. Then came the punchline: "But look what I got!" she would say, as if Ginger was a bad joke. Ginger's mother made Ginger feel like a huge disappointment!

As a wounded child Ginger not only felt unloved, she felt unlovable. She spent a long time believing that and harbored no positive expectations of herself. Her older brothers repeatedly told her she was fat, ugly, and stupid, and Ginger's mother would repeatedly tell her she was uncouth. Ginger internalized all these beliefs, believing them to be true.

Often these rules were reinforced by repeated insults from people who were supposed to love her. There was no one to defend her, and her family's horrid words became rules in Ginger's Internal Rule Book. She remained in this wounded state for a long time, spending many years caught in this self-perpetuating role of impotent victim. In fact, even when someone tried to give Ginger a compliment, she would discard it as a lie. Ginger was powerless to do anything about the situation because her Chatter Mind kept reminding her what was written in her Internal Rule Book. This is often the case with battered women, who remain a victim because they are caught in a web of powerlessness. With Journey Work Ginger improved her self-confidence and changed the beliefs in her Internal Rule Book.

It's often difficult to completely erase a rule from one's Internal Rule Book forever. Perhaps a shadow of the imprint of the rule lies dormant, and at any point the rule may be triggered and revived. In Ginger's case, anything that she considered a "personal failure" could trigger a rule in her Internal Rule Book and reinforce the belief that she was a disappointment and as such, destined to fail.

When I worked with Ginger, she would frequently beat herself up for not meeting expectations and wallow in self-pity, as though never being enough was her destiny. As Ginger cleared her trauma, she became more open to her Soul, which reminded her of her true self and its worth. Real healing always boils down to getting a clear perspective on a situation, without involving the emotions. Always remember that emotions are controlled by the Internal Rule Book and enforced by the Chatter Mind. Just as Ginger benefited from gaining clarity on the contents of her rule book, so did my client Karla, as her case will demonstrate.

Karla Takes On Her Parents' Issues

Karla was an adventurer. She traveled around the world going to exotic places. Even though she was petite, she was fearless. When she met Howard, who was eighteen years her senior, they fell in love. Karla, who had been more or less estranged from her father since her parents divorced when she was a child, was blissfully happy. The night of their rehearsal dinner, however, Karla fell ill with a bizarre ailment; she was dizzy and nauseous.

Karla and Howard married but her nauseous dizziness got worse. Karla tried everything to treat it, but to no avail. This went on for years. When Karla came to see me, we journeyed to find out where her illness had begun. It turned out that in marrying Howard, Karla had significantly changed her lifestyle. Instead of traveling around the world, she now conformed to Howard's more sedentary way of life.

We discovered that, in Karla's Internal Rule Book, Karla had attributed her parents' divorce to their constant separation, given that her father had traveled a great deal. The rule that formed in Karla's rule book might have been, "When one person in a couple travels a lot, the marriage will fall apart." Karla's body got this message loud and clear and tried to help her out by falling ill. In this way she would never be tempted to spend long periods of time away from her husband. Once Karla consciously realized that she would not leave her husband in this way, she became healthier. She had successfully changed an important rule in her Internal Rule Book.

Trudy's Heart Nearly Breaks

If we reside in a situation of dis-ease, it can eventually turn into dis-ease. For afflictions of the heart, it sometimes comes down to having, literally, a broken heart. For example, Trudy, a client of mine, was suffering from A-fib, essentially because she was unable to adjust to her husband Richard's death. They had experienced a great mutual love wherein they cared for each other to the exclusion of the rest of the world; they never had children and lived for each other. In her Internal Rule Book Trudy had written that life without Richard would break her heart. Her bitter loneliness after Richard's death was the cause of her dis-ease, which created her heart disease. When Trudy finally adjusted to Richard's death and started to feel his spiritual presence, she recovered, and her heart was fine. She had successfully changed the rule to include the idea that communication with Richard spiritually could nourish her heart with his love.

Timothy's Perseverance

Timothy wanted to be wealthy and respected. Somehow he had always felt inferior and had been poorly treated by the people around him. In grade school he was the victim of horrible bullying by boys and girls alike. By the time he was in high school he had grown tall and handsome, but he was pigeonholed as a victim by his high school peers. They were not able to see the admirable young man that Timothy had become, and neither was Timothy. It was almost like the lion who grows up with lambs and doesn't realize he's really a lion. As an adult, Timothy pursued success in his professional life, but he was never able to become financially secure. Nevertheless, he struggled on.

After years of personal self-help training Timothy finally had gotten a grip on his finances. A big part of this financial security was due to a job he had. The problem, however, was that he hated this job! Working at what he considered to be menial tasks was embarrassing for him. As a result, while working his day job, he was also creating and building his own company. As that company started to become successful,

Timothy increasingly hated his day job, but because it offered him financial security, he was terrified to leave it.

Spirit heard him and stepped in to make his tenure there horribly uncomfortable, so much so that Timothy could no longer stand the people there, nor the work. Finally his boss, sensitive to Timothy's unhappiness, encouraged him to leave. Timothy almost had a nervous breakdown when he, of his own volition, resigned. Even though his own company was showing increasing glimmers of future success he continued to adhere to his Internal Rule Book, which deemed him to be incompetent. As a result, when he left the security of his day job, Timothy felt extremely vulnerable and very nervous.

Eventually, however, as Timothy witnessed the growth of his own company, he came to have faith in it and himself. In this, he understood that he could create his own financial security doing something he loved. By becoming aware of the many erroneous rules contained in his Internal Rule Book, he was able to overcome them, and he was able to make these changes because he'd spent years trying to understand his Internal Rule Book. Gradually, through personal work with meditation and various forms of energy healing and working with counselors and healers including me, Timothy began to break through the huge wall that prevented him from seeing himself as he truly was.

On one occasion he remembered when he'd participated in the high school debate team and had attended a debate at another school. Given his good looks and charming personality, Timothy was surrounded by girls at that other high school. On the bus ride home, a very popular classmate of Timothy's turned to him and said, "I never realized you were such a chick magnet." This compliment was so different from what Timothy usually heard from members of that group that it made him realize how damaging the opinions of his peer group were to him. He stopped socializing with them and instead began to hang out with younger classmates who were discovering the "new" Timothy.

It was only when Timothy had hit a wall about his horrible job that the Universe had created a work environment so miserable to Timothy that he'd had to leave it. This is spiritual help of the highest order, although it is never really recognized as such. Instead, the forces of the universe that make us take certain actions may be seen as a scourge. It's true that these seeming misfortunes can sometimes break us, which is why we have several Potential Exit Points that are built into our life plan during the Incarnation Planning Time. As I mentioned in chapter 1, these exit points are occasions when we might have an NDE where we can decide to either die or continue living out our life on Earth. These Potential Exit Points are different from our Final Expiration Date that occurs when it's our time for us to leave our present human incarnation.

Jim's Terminal Prison

Jim was working for the family business. He was proud to be following in the footsteps of his father. Jim's position in the company as his father's assistant was golden. He made a very good living and had a wife and three children whom he loved very much, and they loved him too. Everything seemed perfect for Jim in his upper-class life.

When Jim's father fell ill and died, Jim's uncle, who had been more of a silent partner in the company, took over. Jim loathed working for his uncle. It was a living hell for him. He tried to find another job, but he couldn't find anything that would provide his family with the same lifestyle they'd enjoyed for so long.

Jim felt that he needed to suffer along in his current job to provide the standard of living to which his family had become accustomed. In a matter of a few years Jim seemed to fade away. He was always pale and nervous. He never smiled. Jim's work situation was creating dis-ease in his life, which created disease in his body. Although Jim sought out medical attention for his failing body, nothing helped. One day Jim suddenly died. No one was really surprised because Jim had seemed so miserable. Everyone agreed that his job had killed him. And it did.

Jim was caged in by his Internal Rule Book and Chatter Mind. This imprisonment created dis-ease in his life, which eventually led to disease in his body and death. No one has to suffer the way Jim did. We all have the tools necessary to escape the Internal Rule Book and its Chatter Mind cage, but sometimes these tools are not obvious, and it seems the only way out is to suffer until death finally frees us from our prison.

To Be or Not to Be

As we have learned, our Internal Rule Book and Chatter Mind trigger our emotions before our mind can consciously assess a situation. A trauma that created a rule, depending on its severity, can hit us like an emotional tsunami that drowns us in depression. That's why, if anyone around you is talking about suicide, it's extremely important to take that person seriously and help them. Call the Suicide & Crisis Lifeline number at 988.

Suicide is a permanent solution to a temporary problem. We find ourselves believing that, for all kinds of reasons, the world would be better off without us. Remember that the Internal Rule Book is created by personal events, positive and negative, to which value judgments are attached, value judgments that could be completely out of line. In the case of depression, maybe life feels too hard. Maybe we feel abandoned. The situation could be a fatal illness that we can't deal with anymore. Or maybe we can't support ourselves financially, and we will have to depend on others. Perhaps low self-esteem drags us down. Or someone feels that there is no help or hope anywhere.

Because the Internal Rule Book is created spontaneously through our perception of events and is based on visceral experiences, it's hardwired to our emotions and our nervous system. This connection completely bypasses our conscious mind. Again, we experience an emotional reaction to something before we're even consciously aware of what's happening. We see a cute puppy or kitten and feel warmth and love. We see a vicious looking dog and feel afraid. We don't think about what we're experiencing until it's already a perceived reality. We try to learn how to control our emotions, but they all too frequently surface nonetheless.

The more dramatic/traumatic the experience that led to its inclusion in the Internal Rule Book, the stronger the emotional impact. The initial fear, anger, or depression you felt when those rules were created and written in the subconscious mind will indicate the level of emotion you will experience when they're triggered. Because the Internal Rule Book is hardwired to our emotions, a triggered violent emotion can feel like a tsunami. The huge wave of emotion hits us and immediately we find ourselves under water. We don't know which way is up or down.

We continue to lose touch with reality—the reality being that anything is possible—as we drown in the power of this emotional wave. Coherent conscious thought ceases to exist, for the tsunami is too strong. Desperately, as we sink into a pit of depression, everything gets worse, and we can't think straight. As our Soul and spirit guide try to remind us of reasons to live, the waves of emotion drown them out.

Our conscious mind doesn't know what to make of this experience. It's almost as though it ceases to function normally. At this point we may begin to entertain very dark thoughts that lead us to conduct acts of violence, which we probably will later regret. Or perhaps we do the opposite and lose ourselves in a deep depression where suicide becomes a reasonable solution.

For example, suppose we're accustomed to a certain standard of living but are presently having to live a life of reduced circumstances. If we are used to wealth, and our Internal Rule Book says that wealth is good and poverty is bad, then living in poverty can lead to severe depression, which in turn can lead to suicide. Failing health and illness can trigger a belief that our future consists in endless suffering. Or perhaps we've experienced repeated failures—be they professional, social, or romantic—that trigger rules that lead us to believe we are a complete failure and lead us again to depression. Depression is a mindset of hopelessness. We feel we don't belong anymore and, again, we may create a paradigm in our minds where we just don't belong. This is a paradigm where whether we live or die doesn't make any difference to us or especially anyone else, or worse, the world would be better off without us. Chemical imbalance in our body and brain can also throw off our impression of a situation adding to that overwhelming sense of hopelessness. The next few cases will help to shed some light on this troubling subject.

A Victim of Her Internal Rule Book

When I met Diwa, she was an extremely enthusiastic and happy woman. Originally from the Philippines, she was divorced and had pretty much raised her son and daughter as a single mom. When I think of her I remember her broad smile and engaging energy.

Diwa's children were grown up. Her daughter was married and had her own children. She didn't have any time for Diwa. Diwa's son, Damian, didn't settle down as his sister had but enjoyed living and working in New York City. When Diwa's employer forced her to retire, Diwa remained in New York, hoping to find another job. During that time, I rarely saw her. After a few years she excitedly called me to tell me she was moving out West. She had found what she described as a meditation community to join, and she was planning on spending the rest of her life in that community. I was surprised by her bold move, but she spoke about it in such glowing terms that it was impossible to question her decision.

After that, I didn't hear from her. However, one day I ran into Damian, and he told me that Diwa had become disillusioned with the community she'd joined and was considering returning to New York. I was sorry this venture hadn't worked out for her. About a year later Damian called me. Diwa had come back to New York without letting anyone know. She had stayed in a hotel for a few days and then committed suicide. Damian was crushed! He kept asking me why she hadn't called him.

Why didn't Diwa reach out to her loving son? What could have happened to this sunny, happy, and enthusiastic woman that would cause her to take her own life? Diwa had drowned in the tsunami of her depression. She was a victim of her Internal Rule Book. In going out West to join the meditation community she had invested all her meager savings in that organization, which had been a huge mistake. Somehow the members triggered negative aspects of her Internal Rule Book. She had gathered enough energy to escape that community, but when she came back to New York, she had no money and no means of supporting herself. Diwa's self-esteem had taken a huge hit. Now she was so ashamed of her poverty and her error of judgment in joining the group in the first place that she'd been too humiliated to call her children and tell them about her financial situation. She believed that the only way she could survive would be by becoming financially dependent on them, and this was not an option for her.

Drowning in her emotions, I believe that as Diwa sat in her hotel room trying to build up the courage to call her son, her Chatter Mind was having a free-for-all, ruminating on myriad future negative scenarios. These narratives began with her own Internal Rule Book where she berated herself for having made bad choices that proved that she was stupid, and she also harbored the belief that receiving material aid from her children was unforgivable.

As she tried to build up her courage to survive, her Chatter Mind tore her down. Meanwhile her Internal Rule Book was triggering unimaginably strong waves of depression and hopelessness. She was drowning in an emotional tsunami where she couldn't think straight. Hidden away in her hotel room, Diwa took her own life.

Sorina's Downward Slide

Sorina had finally left her abusive husband. She didn't have much money, and her husband was assailing her with many demands through his attorney. The company where Sorina worked had recently downsized and her job had been terminated. At this same time, her daughter, who was in her late teens and bipolar, decided to run away.

The only place Sorina could afford to live was in a sketchy part of town where she was afraid to walk down the street at night. Her world seemed to be crashing down around her. She was filled with anxiety to the point where she began to consider suicide. Although generally a very competent woman full of energy and of a positive nature, all of this was just too much. Sorina couldn't see the end of the tunnel of doom in her life. How had she gotten here?

Anxiety first presents itself when we are emotionally vulnerable and unstable. Leaving her husband was an extremely emotional event for Sorina on many levels, and it had taken incredible personal strength for her to do so. However, in her Internal Rule Book, divorce was considered very bad; therefore Sorina automatically blamed herself for initiating it and completely overlooked that she deserved to escape her abusive husband. That said, Sorina hadn't realized that leaving the marriage would create such heavy financial problems for herself. On top of it all, her daughter showered Sorina with outrageous disparaging remarks.

All this triggered the emotion of anger at what she considered to be her own stupidity. Already carrying the burden of guilt, the fact that Sorina's daughter had run away triggered a belief in her Internal Rule Book that told her that this outcome involving her daughter was directly linked to Sorina's inability to be a proper mother. The emotion attached to this idea was devastating. Although the loss of her job had nothing to do with her job performance or her personally, Sorina blamed herself for what she perceived to be the poor choices she'd made in her professional life, which had resulted in her current unemployed status. Her situation also triggered her to fall into a deep depression. Feeling low and lost, Sorina became fearful of her surroundings and refused all offers of help. Thoughts of suicide again entered her mind.

The key to Sorina's recovery was for her to find rays of positivity amid the gloom. Her grown son, who had been away, returned. Having witnessed his father's abuse toward his mother, the son showed Sorina *a great deal of support. He also congratulated Sorina for her escape from the abusive marriage. This positive reinforcement of her situation triggered Sorina's Internal Rule Book to remind her of how she had been an outstanding mother to her son and daughter. She began to realize that her daughter was fraught with mental issues that, in retrospect, Sorina had been dealing with for years as Sorina tried to find help for her daughter. Sorina's Internal Rule Book, with its registry of all events good and bad, brought forth the necessary positive events that allowed her to build a literal lifeline.*

As Sorina's story demonstrates, our emotions may come on so quickly and forcefully that it may be difficult to stop them. The tsunami of feelings can flood our being, and it is in these moments of hopelessness that our energy leaves us, like the air escaping a balloon that's been pierced. Without energy we truly cannot function except possibly to commit suicide to end the pain. Whenever anyone is in an emotional tsunami of depression, it's tremendously important to just wait it out. It will pass. Stay in a fetal position in bed if need be. Trust that the tsunami will pass and you will see a better day.

The truth is, though, that after experiencing an emotional tsunami and coming out the other side, we might look back and wonder how we could have been so ridiculous as to even consider suicide, much less act on it. Once we're able to distance ourselves from our emotions, our energy returns, and we are able to consciously examine a situation and be reminded of positive, lifesaving events in our Internal Rule Book. We begin to hear our Soul and spirit guides. Is it really hopeless? They can be helpful by communicating with us to give us a different perspective, triggering more positive entries in our Internal Rule Book and showing us a positive path forward.

Alice Seeks a Way Out

Alice was a therapist who loved her job and her clients. Her relationship with her husband, however, was going from bad to worse. When they split up, Alice found herself alone and penniless thanks to her husband's financial mismanagement. After years of trying to make it on her own, however, Alice had managed to afford her own apartment and was able to support herself.

This was like a house of cards, though, because Alice lived hand to mouth. Every month was a struggle to pay the rent and any major financial surprise would upset the whole structure.

The day came when Alice's old car needed some very expensive repairs, which would upset her fragile financial stability. Alice had felt very clever when she managed to lease a brand-new car that didn't break her bank. This was a great workaround to her mechanical car problems and was just the car she wanted.

Then one day someone drove into her new car and totaled it. The good news was that Alice wasn't in or near the car. The bad news was that the insurance would cover the cost of the car, paying it off to the leasing company, but leaving Alice with nothing.

It seemed that Alice would have to ask someone for money; money she thought she would never be able to return. Alice hated the whole situation. Feelings of being drowned washed over her, but she couldn't verbalize them; they were so overwhelming. Alice was caught in an emotional tsunami. She began to think about suicide because she couldn't stand being in such a cash-strapped situation anymore. She felt abused by life, and she couldn't take another day. She began to imagine ways to commit suicide. She thought of stepping in front of a moving car.

For a moment Alice wondered if she might survive an accident and then have an even more miserable life. As the emotional tsunami hit her again, Alice felt an urgency to end it all with more certainty. It never entered Alice's mind that her suicide could be damaging to her children. Sobbing and feeling entirely alone and hopeless Alice tripped and fell, severely injuring her right leg. It was at this point that I found her on the ground as I was walking my dog. I worked with Alice and as a result, she seemed to get a grip on herself and come out of the emotional tsunami. I connected her with her spirit guides who were trying to get her attention. It's possible that they made her trip.

As we talked, she began to realize the folly of killing herself and the huge damage it would do to her children. She pulled herself together. With encouragement from her Soul and spirit guides Alice went on to borrow some money from a friend and managed to get a car. Her friend was very gracious and understanding and could easily afford to loan Alice the money. Alice's triumph in securing a car made her much stronger and bolstered her self-esteem. She had survived the weak moments and the suicidal thoughts. She opened up to her spirit guides and managed to change a few rules in her Internal Rule Book in the process.

The Universe Makes a Point

While I was writing the previous section on suicide, it came time for my monthly Mediumship Group at the New Dawn Foundation. The whole idea of suicide was so sad that I was glad to get away from it for a few hours. During these mediumship meetings, we, as a group, contact a deceased person in an effort to bring comfort to an attendee who was missing their loved one.

I enjoy my Mediumship Group very much because every time I go, I meet new people and reconnect with a few regulars. For this particular meeting there were many new people who didn't know each other. All of them had loved ones they wanted to contact, and all of the deceased had committed suicide.

As I contacted the spirits for the grieving attendees, each spirit indicated that they had no idea they would be missed. More than that, they didn't realize the pain they had caused people they loved. Across the board, for different reasons and in different ways, they committed suicide, believing that they were ridding the world of a toxic person—themselves. Their methods of committing suicide were all different, but they all explained how they were in the depths *of despair and had to get out. They were drowning in an emotional tsunami and couldn't see anything but the pain they could no longer tolerate. It's obvious to me that Spirit arranged this special Mediumship Group so that I could pass on this important message: let people know how much you care about them. Never hesitate to tell someone, "You're a great person." You just might be saving their life.*

5

The Internal Rule Book as We Age

THE PROCESS OF RECORDING RULES in our Internal Rule Book starts when we are very young and continues throughout our lives. As we established in previous chapters, event + rule entry = emotional and physical reaction. So as we live our daily life and go through the many different changes brought about as we age, all of those events are stored in our Internal Rule Book with a judgment added to each event, which in turn triggers an emotion. When a similar event happens later in our lives, those emotions are triggered, and we act—or react—according to our Internal Rule Book. We follow these rules out of habit and fear. After all, the Internal Rule Book is there to protect us, so if we don't follow its dictates we risk physical or emotional injury. On our own we don't have the mental acuity to review and change the rules that are in our Internal Rule Book.

Pricilla and Her Fear of Sex

Pricilla was a lovely twenty-eight-year-old woman. She told me that she had been dating the same guy for four years and they'd been discussing marriage and having children. She was concerned about getting married, though, because she'd never had sex. Soon after she had met her boyfriend, Alfred, she fell ill with what doctors diagnosed as Lyme disease. She had been terribly sick in many inexplicable ways. Alfred had been with her the whole time. She was finally healed at a Christian church. As Pricilla opened up to me she shared that she was afraid to have sex.

She had been nervous about having a session because she'd had a session with a medium a couple of years prior that was horribly disturbing. Apparently the medium had told her that her father had molested her when she was young, and she needed to see a therapist. Obviously this news was horrific. Shortly after that Pricilla fell ill. I suggested that we do some Journey Work to find out why she had issues with sex. She was concerned that she would find some bad things about her life, so I explained to her that in the way that I do Journey Work she would not feel the emotions. I explained that sometimes past-life experiences can influence us in our current life.

We began the Journey Work and everything was going well. I always begin in a soothing, happy place. Our mission was to find out why Pricilla was so afraid of sex. Pricilla volunteered that she especially didn't like the penis. The first thing she described was herself as an infant, maybe three or four months old. She said that there was a monster above her that frightened her. I cleared that away for her. The next scene she described was when she was five or six. She found herself in a jungle and seemed to hear the word grandfather. First a dark shape appeared and turned into a man who was holding what looked like a huge, dead snake. She seemed to hear something about how she shouldn't tell anyone about this. She felt frightened. I asked if she was supposed to touch the snake, and she said yes.

I asked if she was supposed to do more with the snake. She wasn't able to answer this clearly but said that she felt the answer was yes. I cleared this experience and brought her back to the happy place. Then I asked her about her grandfathers. One was alive, and the other was dead. She didn't have any conscious memory of anything happening with either one, so she decided that this had been a past-life experience.

Upon recognizing the source of her fear, she felt detached from it and ready to get married and have a family.

It is possible that Pricilla's original trauma came from a past life, one where she was in a jungle. But there was definitely a current-incarnation trauma of sexual abuse that triggered that past-life memory. Luckily, Pricilla didn't need all the details to rid herself of this trauma.

Pricilla's childhood experience of being sexually abused—remembered or not—was recorded in her Internal Rule Book. As a result, she was afraid of a penis to the extent that when she was with a man with whom she wanted to be intimate, she fell ill. Her Internal Rule Book sent out the emotion of fear, which created so much dis-ease for her that she actually contracted a disease.

Adolescence to Midlife

As teenagers we question everything and, in so doing, we are apt to challenge the status quo. This is when our Internal Rule Book takes a hit. The control of the Internal Rule Book over our emotions and actions is overruled by the huge waves of hormones running through us. Our emotions become an electrical system that is constantly running near overload and often shorts out. The result can be incredible mood swings and outbursts, bizarre and risky behavior, and confusion. The difficult part for the Soul is that the physical demands of life seem to cut off communication between the Soul and the physical body. Generally there is some detachment between the two.

Teenage energy levels are also all over the map. Marathons of sleeplessness are mixed with days of never getting up except under duress. This affects not only the teenager but also anyone who has to deal with the teenager. The effect is palpable and radiates out like ripples in a lake, often making other people begin to question their own Internal Rule Book. During this difficult time there are many rules entered in a teenager's rule book that are generated by their "loving" parents or caretakers who often inadvertently say and do hurtful things. Unfortunately, words uttered in anger write the more indelible rules in our Internal Rule Books. Although the parents or caregivers receive their share of negative entries, the teenager gets the brunt of it. Something as simple as "You're lazy!" will be registered in the Internal Rule Book and down the road will affect the teenager's self-esteem.

Dr. Jekyll and Mr. Hyde

Lucy was a good mother to her teenage son Luke. He was a handsome boy who was happy and pleasant with others. He was good at making jokes and enjoyed company, especially that of his family. One day Lucy and Luke went shopping together. Lucy noticed that Luke was consistently out of step with her, walking either in front of her or behind her. As Lucy tried harder to keep up with Luke, she realized he was purposely avoiding walking next to her. "Why?" she asked him.

"I don't know. I just don't want to walk next to you," Luke answered from behind Lucy.

This was only part of a new unpleasant Luke who seemed to have taken over the old, adorable Luke. This new version refused to do anything he was asked to do. The minimal chores he was supposed to do became reasons for battle. Lucy found herself trying to avoid asking Luke anything because he was so unpleasant. Luke had become an equal opportunity dispenser of his unpleasantness. His father was also a recipient of this alienation, as were his siblings.

Luke now always complained about everything. He made life miserable for everyone in the family. Lucy and her husband tried everything to understand and try to help Luke but to no avail. The new Luke seemed to be a permanent fixture in their home now. Months passed, and no one could remember the wonderful, pleasant Luke who used to belong to their family.

One day Lucy's daughter came running up to her. "Mom, look! Luke is bringing in the garbage can from the street! And you didn't even ask him to do it!" Lucy had to see this with her own eyes. Bringing in the empty garbage can was Luke's chore, but he hadn't done it in at least a year without an argument with either his father or Lucy. When Luke came into the house, Lucy thanked him for bringing in the garbage can. Luke looked at her and smiled and said, "You're welcome." Lucy couldn't believe it. Who was this nice stranger? As the evening progressed Luke was the sweet old Luke again.

Wanting to reinforce his positive behavior, Lucy said, "Luke, you're being so nice."

Luke said, "Yeah."

"You haven't been so nice lately," Lucy said hesitantly, believing he might not have realized this.

"Yeah, I know."

Lucy was dumbfounded. Luke knew he'd been unpleasant and rude. "Why were you being so unpleasant?"

"I don't know."

It's fortunate that Lucy didn't know of all the risky and often stupid things Luke had done over the previous year, like climbing out of his window at night to meet his friends, experimenting with alcohol, driving on a frozen lake . . .

The answer to Luke's behavior is that his hormones were flooding his brain and short-circuiting his Internal Rule Book. All the rules about how he should act and the fear of consequences for not doing so were thrown out the window. His world was turned upside down. In this state he was deaf to his own rule book and deaf to his Soul.

When teenagers go through hormonal upheavals and question everything, their parents may be forced to examine things too, but for different reasons. After spending many years raising a child, parents are unprepared for teenagers who challenge their parents' choices. The chosen method of this challenge is criticism. Because a teenager is capable of speaking like an adult about adult topics, parents can be fooled into believing that their child really has grown up. This is not entirely true. A teenager is like a rose bush that has many buds, but only a few are blooming now. Later on the bush will be in full bloom. You also have to watch out for the thorns.

The comments that a teenager can make about a parent's job can lead a parent to question not only their job choice but also all the choices they've made since they were teenagers themselves. As the teenager is becoming an adult, the role of the parent is changing. As all this change and introspection are happening, the Internal Rule Book gets overruled and modified for the parents too.

Due to the physical changes that teenagers go through during adolescence, they can be huge catalysts for their parents to modify their own Internal Rule Book. The problem comes when each of their Internal Rule Books records all the negative interactions between parent and teen. If we aren't careful these entries can create horrible fodder for the Chatter Mind that can destabilize both parent and child.

Most of us want to get older until we hit twenty-one. Then we want to stay young. After the tumultuous teenage years, our Internal Rule Book becomes more stable, but the emotional punch gets stronger. It's interesting how reflecting on our age is integrated into our Internal Rule Book, so our emotions are triggered by turning thirty; we consider that we are getting old. It is a landmark age that is defined by our Internal Rule Book. Depending on our previous entries, we can consider that we are doing very well or not. Gradually our Internal Rule Book gets a better hold on our emotions, and we generate habits. The more habits we create, the more we build an Internal Rule Book/Chatter Mind cage. By forty we are fairly set in our ways.

At this point in our lives, Internal Rule Book challenges are difficult to face. We are better at outwardly controlling our emotions, but our Internal Rule Book is even more adept at triggering these emotions. In our forties, early childhood traumas, which have been buried from our conscious mind, may begin to surface. This happens now because we are in a better position to face these significant traumas and gain the understanding that the trauma was supposed to bring us. It's important to remember at this point that we planned these traumas in our lives. We plan these challenges as learning opportunities.

When I was in my forties it was as though the rose-colored glasses were ripped off my face. If long before Wassim hadn't brought into my consciousness that childhood car accident where we drove off a cliff and fell 135 feet, that memory would have begun to break through to me at this point. The reality of the sexual abuse I suffered as a three- and four-year-old came into my awareness. I believe in my case, I needed to take control of that abuse and realize that I could prevent anything like that ever happening to me again. At that point I was also opening up to spirit communication, which helped me deal with what I was uncovering. We all have our spirit guides there to help us during this time. Later on I realized that as a healer, I could empathize better with my clients thanks to the fact that I had suffered this kind of abuse.

These traumas are revealed so late in our lives because we are better able to deal with them and learn from them. If we don't deal with them in the present incarnation, we will surely face similar trauma in the next incarnation.

Throughout our fifties there is a continuation of our development and more opportunities to develop our connection to spirits. There is a sense of needing to live life as our bodies begin to show signs of slowing down. If we don't learn how to fill ourselves with energy, we are in trouble.

Turning fifty is an especially important time for women. As menopause hovers, women receive a download of wisdom. This is a kind of spiritual opening that wasn't accessible at a younger age. This wisdom helps women to question their Chatter Mind, their belief system, and their Internal Rule Book.

Retirement

In our sixties we are forced to change some rules because we have to deal with retirement. As much as we loathe having to change, now we must, for the circumstances demand it. Retirement is usually seen as a wonderful reward following a life of hard work. In addition to the financial considerations that can dictate when someone might retire, there are emotional components that often are ignored. We know when we've had enough of a job, and we feel ready to leave it.

Unfortunately, we don't always plan our retirement well. Even if we are financially sound and have wonderful plans to build our forever home or travel extensively or possibly both, we forget about our Internal Rule Book. The rules in it, which we've set up unconsciously throughout our lives, are hardwired to our emotions. This means that even if we are finally vacationing on that sunny beach in Tahiti, something may be bothering us.

Usually we can't identify it, and we simply ignore it. Our conscious mind convinces us that we're happy. The pernicious quality of the Internal Rule Book never stops working, however. If our Internal Rule Book has identified success and happiness as a hardworking adult, we won't be able to be happy without some component of that hardworking adult in our lives. The more successful and well connected someone has been in their life, the more severe the consequences can be.

Those consequences cause dis-ease and illness. We go from being perceived as someone whose decisions make a difference and whose calls are immediately answered to someone less important. Eventually this leads to becoming someone who is ill and reliant on caregivers to survive. One way to mitigate this outcome is to prepare your retirement by finding some kind of charity organization to join and give you a voice. The best result is when the level of your stature within the charity corresponds to the level of professional responsibility that you had before you retired. Although there is a huge step between paid work and benevolent charity work, the Internal Rule Book will still perceive the charity work as satisfying its definition of success. Finally, you will be able to fully enjoy that vacation in Tahiti as it's attached to a Doctors Without Borders outpost that you're supposed to visit.

My Father's Retirement

My father had a long, successful career as an engineer. He loved his work, especially when he was in charge of the overhaul of several steel plants. We were all invited to visit the renovated steel plants when the work was done. My dad retired, ready to enjoy lots of time in Florida. The problem was that my mother, nine years his junior, was still working. Together they decided it would be best to postpone that move to Florida for a few years. That turned out to be a bad decision. Although Dad had a lot of fix-it projects around the house, without his professional job or any other commitment that needed his expertise where he could meet with people, he soon fell ill with one thing after another. His dis-ease turned into disease. Eventually my parents scrapped their plans to move to Florida because they wanted to stay near Dad's doctors.

It was tremendously sad to see my father turn into a shell of his former self. He was a very brave and good man. One of my final memories of him was our last Thanksgiving dinner. He loved to eat! But now he was being fed through a tube in his stomach. He had esophageal cancer. He sat there at the table, smiling, laughing, and enjoying the family gathering and the smell of the copious Thanksgiving dinner.

Dad's Internal Rule Book contained rules that described his personal self-worth. Obviously an important rule was his work ethic and the importance of being a productive worker. I can't help but wonder if Dad had gotten involved in some sort of organization—like Habitat for Humanity where he could have used his skills as an engineer and felt like a productive part of society—whether he could have avoided so much illness.

Elderhood

The positive side of growing older is that we react more slowly to the emotions triggered by our Internal Rule Book. We might experience an emotion longer, but our physical reactions are delayed—except those triggered by depression, which can creep in. Somehow, we become more philosophical, and we might temper our emotions. This continues through old age. We have a choice to become bitter; that is, horribly cantankerous if not downright mean, or better; that is, more forgiving and generous. These results depend on the input each individual enters into the Internal Rule Book. It's a good idea to review the contents of your Internal Rule Book to prepare to be a better elder.

As people live longer, it seems that the key is acceptance of what is. In a sense, this is a newfound ability to not take issue with events when our Internal Rule Book triggers our emotions. The people who live the longest generally are those who roll with the punches in life. Of course having a strong connection to your Soul and spirits helps in this process.

6

The Positive and Negative of the Internal Rule Book and Chatter Mind

SOMETIMES IT MAY SEEM like our Internal Rule Book and Chatter Mind are only interested in reining us in and preventing us from enjoying life. When we realize that the Internal Rule Book's foremost goal is to protect us, then the idea of a doom and gloom "Internal Rule Book prison" with its haunting guard Chatter Mind becomes more understandable.

I can hear you thinking, *What about the emotional tsunami that's triggered by our Internal Rule Book? How is that supposed to protect us?* The emotion is supposed to highlight something important. The tsunami of emotion is supposed to sweep us away to impulsive action that could be positive: *Yes, I'm going to propose marriage! Yes, I'm going to risk my life to save that child!* Or negative: *I don't want to be the laughingstock! I might as well quit!*

As we were growing up there were lots of adults telling us what we should do—and more often what we shouldn't do. "Don't touch the stove." "Don't run down the stairs." "Don't push others." "Don't hit." "Wait." "Stop yelling." "Stop crying." You get the point. Our Internal

Rule Book adds all this to its "help list" of rules. Then our Chatter Mind gets busy generously applying the words *stop*, *don't*, *wait* to all we do, and constantly reminds us, "You're bad!" "You don't understand anything!" "You're impossible!"

One of my mother's favorites for me was, "I hope you have a daughter like you! That'll be your real punishment!" The truth is, however, I have two amazing daughters who are absolutely perfect in every way! Thankfully my self-esteem, which took a hit from my mother's harsh words—written into my Internal Rule Book and mercilessly repeated to me throughout the years by my Chatter Mind—wasn't completely destroyed. Our Internal Rule Book and Chatter Mind seem to emphasize the negative because their job is to keep us safe by either sweeping us into action or preventing us from moving too quickly. Highlighting potential negative outcomes is in their job description as our protectors, and they'll keep at it until we decide we've had enough.

The Gift of Gratitude

One way to control our Internal Rule Book and Chatter Mind is to express gratitude. As we force ourselves to identify what we're grateful for, our Internal Rule Book and Chatter Mind are listening. They already have a list of their own. In addition, if you've ever experienced making a list of things you're grateful for, you might have noticed that in no time that list gets very long. Instead of focusing on all that isn't right in your life, changing your aim to focus on what is right can lead to a change in personal perception, which may lead to a real boost in self-esteem and energy as the Internal Rule Book records it all.

This is not unlike constructing a building, wherein it's important to have a clear, solid foundation. If we're riddled with self-doubt it's like trying to build success on top of failure. Identifying what is right in your life and expressing your appreciation for that makes your foundation strong and positive. Anything you do from there has a much better chance of success. The best part is that when we surround ourselves with that positive feeling of all that is good in our lives, our Chatter Mind joins the chorus.

Michèle's Surprising Return

Michèle Bögli-Mastria had an NDE, which she describes as a beautiful experience. On her twenty-first birthday she was scheduled to go on a company retreat. Michèle was in perfect health; however, both her father and her grandmother were in the hospital, which worried her a great deal. During her retreat with her colleagues, Michèle experienced pain in her kidneys and blood in her urine. At first she thought it was a urinary tract infection and decided she would see a doctor when she got home. When the pain became unbearable to the point that she was screaming, an ambulance was called and she went to the emergency room. In the ambulance they gave her an IV. Waiting in the ER for an ultrasound, still in excruciating pain, she began to feel very strange.

After a while a nurse walked in and blanched when she looked at her. "Don't look down," the nurse said and quickly left the room. Shortly later a doctor came in and also blanched as he too told her not to look down. The IV had ruptured so that rather than fill her with liquid it had been leaking her blood out. The doctor walked out of the room and began yelling for help. At this point Michèle did look down and saw blood everywhere. She didn't realize she was bleeding out as they took her to another part of the hospital where she was surrounded by curtains.

She was in a tremendous amount of pain as she waited. Then suddenly, the pain stopped as she felt washed in beautiful pure light that felt like unconditional love. It was difficult for her to find words to express what she experienced. She noticed a white hazy entity, an angel, to her left. With the angel she visited her earthly life to say goodbye. This was when she realized that she was dying, which didn't bother her at all because where she was felt so good. Suddenly she felt a bang and horrendous pain, and she realized that she was back in her body. She hadn't wanted to come back; she just did.

When she returned to life, Michèle had a great deal of difficulty adjusting. It seemed that Michèle's Internal Rule Book and Chatter Mind were dragging her into depression. The negative comments of her Chatter Mind were a reflection of the accumulation of rules that had stifled her after she'd experienced the vast freedom of the spirit world. During her NDE, Michèle's spirit had been ready to leave that pain-filled body, but the Creator clearly had other ideas. Michèle's time on earth was not finished. She still needed to learn more.

However, depressed and unable to cope, Michèle started drinking, often becoming completely drunk. One morning she found herself drunk again. She began to question why she was alive. Why had she been sent back? What was the point? She heard a voice say, "Find gratitude."

In the beginning she forced herself to find something to be grateful about, for she didn't really feel grateful at all. Every night, she gave thanks regardless. Gradually she found more and more things to appreciate about her life. Soon very mundane things and events were on her gratitude list.

When hearing that she should find gratitude from such a powerful voice, Michèle's Soul had been emboldened enough to cajole her into noticing the good aspects of her life. In this way Michèle was learning what she needed to learn while she was incarnate. She was able to add so many positive entries to her Internal Rule Book that her Chatter Mind would remind her of these rather than the horrors she had previously been hearing.

The Gift of Pain

One of the reasons our Internal Rule Book and Chatter Mind have such control over us is that we recognize that together they can protect us from pain. Our Internal Rule Book is largely built on rules that help us avoid suffering. This can include not only physical suffering but emotional pain as well. Fear of any kind of pain is a great motivator.

Why is there pain in such a beautiful world? If there is a benevolent greater power who created our lives, why do pain and suffering exist? What we call suffering or looking into the abyss or a dark night of the Soul is required for a full incarnate experience.

Accordingly, when someone is having their difficult time in life, they are supposed to have it. Only by "suffering" and getting through it, will they be stronger and more fulfilled when their perceived problem is resolved, and they move on to life's next challenge. In many cases this is a matter of erasing chapters from their Internal Rule Book and changing their Chatter Mind monologue. It is important for all of us to show compassion and help someone going through a difficult time. We all experience this more or less. It can be excruciating and debilitating, so it is extremely important to help anyone going through this.

The Pain of Estrangement

Sometimes we bring pain into our lives to achieve a goal. Fred was in his late fifties when he came to see me. Fred had been married for several years and had a son and a daughter. The marriage was not going well and Fred's wife had an affair and got pregnant by her lover. Fred found out and in disgust left his wife. She, however, never told anyone that she was pregnant by another man. Fred was considered the evil person for leaving a pregnant wife. Fred just left and didn't communicate with her or their friends anymore. As a result his wife's family treated him like dirt, and he had little access to his children. Not wanting to make the situation worse, Fred never told anyone that his wife's third child was from a different father.

After many years of being estranged from his kids, Fred tried to reconcile with them as they began to reach adulthood. His daughter and his wife's daughter, who was fathered by another man and never knew that Fred was not her biological father, responded to him. Fred's son refused to have anything to do with him, however, which destroyed Fred. He fell ill with cancer, subconsciously hoping that his son would then come to him. The son did not.

During this time Fred met a beautiful woman, and they fell in love. His love for her sparked in Fred a true desire to live, and his cancer went into remission. He was cancer free. Fred tried again to contact his son but with no success. His two daughters, especially the one who was not his biological daughter, doted on him. This bothered Fred tremendously, and he wanted the whole story of his wife's infidelity and lies to come out. His ex-wife pressured Fred not to tell the illegitimate daughter about the circumstances of her birth because she had just begun to recover from the pain of feeling abandoned by her father—who she believed to be Fred.

I worked with Fred. During our sessions he would improve when I brought in the love energy he shared with his girlfriend. Fred would leave my office and be fine. A few months later, however, he'd be sick again. This back-and-forth happened several times. Eventually Fred stopped seeing me. He gave up and no longer tried to recover. Fred was subconsciously using his illness to try to reconnect with his son but, unfortunately, that didn't work, and Fred died.

Sometimes we experience pain to help us open up to our spirit connection. This is what happened to the nineteenth-century figure Saint Bernadette of Lourdes. Bernadette was badly treated in a convent where the head nun would make her spend hours every day in a cold stone cell on her knees praying, a position made all the more painful by her rheumatoid arthritis. But Bernadette welcomed the pain and was grateful for it because she said it brought her closer to God.

Saint John of the Cross had a similar story. A priest during the Spanish Inquisition, he was imprisoned in a small closet and was taken out only to be beaten. It was in this closet that he had an epiphany in which he felt he'd made a real connection with God. After that he miraculously escaped and wrote his most beautiful poetry.

While a positive outcome from pain and suffering may seem like a paradox, it's only because we don't understand that we experience pain not to suffer but to learn. Padre Pio, the nineteenth-century Italian

Franciscan Capuchin, friar, priest, and mystic, shared this parable: There was a young boy who, from his vantage point, could only see the threads of the embroidery that his mother was working on, and he wondered why she would spend so much time on something so ugly. Then one day his mother tilted the embroidery so that he could see its beautiful pattern.

The Creator is benevolent. Pain is a part of learning and is but one thread in the tapestry of life.

The Gift of Disease

There are many reasons for disease. The one most pertinent to the Internal Rule Book and Chatter Mind begins with the creation of a personal state of dis-ease. This happens when the Internal Rule Book establishes our rules to live by, at the same time keeping a tally of our personally defined successes and especially our failures. The Chatter Mind broadcasts these failures incessantly to us in order to motivate us. However, that can and usually does backfire, and the Chatter Mind can trigger our emotions such that we may fall into a depressed state. Life is not happening the way we want it to. Maybe we are alone, and we want to be married. Maybe we are married and hate our spouse. Maybe our house is too small. Maybe we can't afford a house. Maybe we can't afford food. Maybe we hate our job. You get the picture.

Georgia Postpones Her Marriage

Georgia was a beautiful young woman in her midtwenties. She was in love with her wonderful boyfriend, James, who seemed intent on getting engaged. The problem was that Georgia was very sick. Her symptoms resembled lupus but not conclusively. Georgia wanted to get rid of her mystery illness before taking another step forward in her life. To help with this, Georgia came to see me.

During her Journey Work session, I took Georgia to the origins of her illness. Georgia began remembering when she worked at a restaurant when she was a junior in high school. There she became friends with one of the cooks, Craig. He was in his twenties. They got along well as friends and laughed a lot. One evening Craig invited Georgia to his house. For Georgia, Craig was like a big brother, and she felt safe with him. During the Journey Work the next thing Georgia remembered was waking up in the early morning on Craig's bed, fully dressed. She hurried home feeling really confused. It was not her style to sleep over at a random place. Craig said she had fallen asleep, and he just put her on his bed so she could sleep better. Nothing had happened sexually because she was still fully dressed.

Nevertheless Georgia kept talking about how strange that was; not the least bit like her. I journeyed back with Georgia to when she arrived at Craig's house. She had never been there before. She and Craig were laughing and talking as they drank some beer. I asked Georgia to watch what happened as an observer. She saw herself pass out, and then she saw Craig undress her and have sex with her. She was a virgin. He then cleaned her up and redressed her. Georgia was horrified. Craig must have drugged her! This seemed to explain to Georgia why she didn't experience the typical signs of being a virgin when she had had sex with James who she thought to be her first sex partner. I cleared the energy for Georgia and she felt lighter.

As the days passed, Georgia recovered from her illness. She broke up with James, realizing that she needed to process the trauma she discovered she had experienced. As Georgia threw herself into her studies and her career, avoiding anything to do with men, her symptoms cleared up. I told Georgia that she would meet someone in her profession who she would marry. Sure enough, a few years later Georgia met Gary. They fell in love and married. Once Georgia realized that her Internal Rule Book wouldn't allow her to marry James because of the trauma she had experienced, she reconciled the trauma and rewrote the rules. Putting herself in a situation of professional power, she was ready to handle risking a relationship.

Jill Bypasses Her Chatter Mind

My client Jill grew up in a community where she didn't really fit in. She always felt like a lower-class, poor person. Although she loved her family and they loved her, there were problems. Her father was an angry man and took it out on Jill. He would occasionally beat her when he decided she wasn't following his orders. Jill was in a hurry to get out of the house. She married her high school boyfriend, but in a few years realized that with him she was building the same poor life she had left. Jill dreamed of being high-society rich.

When Jill met Don she saw a man who represented high society and old money. It wasn't long before Jill got a divorce and married Don. With this, she entered the upper class. Jill had three children and was living a happy life. Things were going well, and her children were in high school and college when Don ran into a difficult situation at work. Because of changes in the company his income was cut substantially.

Suddenly Jill had to worry about money. As she became very upset at the idea of losing her status, she was diagnosed with cancer. Jill had become caged in by her Internal Rule Book and her Chatter Mind, which constantly reminded her of the misery she'd felt growing up being poor and not fitting in. She had worked so hard to arrive, and now all was lost!

She also felt that Don wasn't working hard enough to fight for what he was entitled to receive. He would come home every night and recount to her the horrors of his day. When this happened, Jill, a street fighter, would think about how she would have handled the situation. She was furious at what she considered to be the wimpy manner in which Don was attempting to stand his ground, but there was nothing she could do about it.

After going through surgery and then months of chemotherapy, Jill turned to religion and prayer. She worked with me to gain a different perspective and bypass her Chatter Mind. Once she did this, she was able to control her Chatter Mind. Then together we journeyed to *access her Internal Rule Book so we could change some of the rules it contained.*

Today Jill is cancer free and is living happily with Don and their children.

The Gifts of Pleasure and Humor

Depending on our Internal Rule Book and any karmic baggage, our enjoyment of pleasure can be dampened to the point of extinction. Our Internal Rule Book doesn't always concur with our current beliefs. This can color the quality of any pleasurable event or even how we might define pleasure. Is pleasure just a matter of feeling good? Or is it a sense of accomplishment? Whether we're receiving an award or a simple smile from our own child, our Chatter Mind can prevent us from taking in the pleasure of the moment.

And that's what it's all about. The pleasure of the moment. People who age well and live beyond a hundred seem to have a special component in their outlook on life: a definition of pleasure that mutes or erases the memories of sadness. My son Terence has the ability to make people laugh. It's a wonderful gift that I've seen transform a depressed person into a cheerful one. Our many philosophical discussions have helped me stay positive when I'm dealing with the subject of death and dying almost on a daily basis.

There is humor to be found anywhere and everywhere; it's often just a matter of seeking it out. The movie *Life Is Beautiful*, wherein a father and son are in a concentration camp, speaks to this point. The father creates the illusion for his son that they are just at a strange and funny retreat.

At my Mediumship Group we almost always end up laughing together. It's as though Spirit brings joy into our gathering. People who are connecting to a loved one who they miss so much end up smiling and laughing as the spirit of that person reminds them of happy times.

We can learn so much from trees. A tree just is. Given the right conditions of soil, light, and water, it will grow into whatever kind of tree it is. As life's challenges hit it, it steadily continues growing for as long as it can. A lack of water, nutrients, sun, or disease can afflict the tree, but nevertheless it continues to grow as much as it can. And it never questions what kind of tree it is. It just follows its mission to fully become whatever kind of tree it is meant to be.

We humans are more complicated by our Internal Rule Book and Chatter Mind. Rather than allowing ourselves to grow following our talents and our preferences, we question it all. For example, rather than simply exploring our talents and identifying our preferences, we take hold of what should be a natural process and complicate it. If we were in the tree world, we would decide, or allow others to decide for us, what kind of tree we should become. Maybe an oak tree for instance? The problem arises when genetically and spiritually we're wired to become a plum tree and not an oak. We wouldn't be very happy being relatively small and having purple things hanging off our branches.

In the same way, rather than simply allowing themselves to experience pleasure as it comes up, many people make it a commodity over which they allow their minds to take control. This begins when we are young children.

Sally Sabotages Her Own Happiness

Sally was turning seven and planning a birthday party. Mom and Dad were on board and the party planning was going well. It would be just the kind of party Sally had always dreamed of. Meanwhile Sally's best friend, Anna, began to shut Sally out. Poor Sally suffered a lot because of this. Finally, Anna told Sally that her party was stupid, and she was not going to attend because there was something else she wanted to do that would be more fun. Sally was crushed.

The party began and Sally started to cry. All the party preparations and the many other children who had shown up for it didn't mean a thing to Sally. She failed to see the pleasure in her party because *she was grieving about her friend. It didn't help to know that Anna had acted the way she had because she was jealous of Sally and her party. Sally had decided that her party was only going to be a success if Anna was there. How often do we define the happiness of an event by expectations that we create rather than by being open to whatever might happen? It's tremendously important to avoid expectations!*

Carl Holds Back

Carl was thirty years old. By this point in his life he had experienced some rejection from girls in high school and college. Finally he met a woman to whom he was very attracted. Rather than allow himself to enjoy the excitement of falling in love, however, Carl held back his feelings, waiting for something negative to happen. Being repressed, Carl missed the pleasure of the moment, probably scaring this woman away. Carl came to me when he was teetering on falling in love. He was terrified to the point of being ill. Carl's new love, Samantha, was a wonderful woman who was kind and patient with Carl. Working with me Carl was able to overcome his fear of rejection and failure and show his love for Samantha. They eventually married and are happy together.

Carol Can't See the Forest for the Trees

Carol was forty-five and an empty nester who'd lost interest in her marriage and could no longer derive pleasure from it. Nor could she even feel happy that she was married. Her children had developed their own independent lives, and on top of it all, Carol worked at a job she hated. If she could take a break from her Chatter Mind, which was constantly repeating to her what a miserable situation she was in, she'd be able to indulge in some of life's simple joys and pleasures. Carol came to me, and using Journey Work, I was able to show her all that was good in her life. She could also see what action she could take to be happier. As part of her session, I gave her energy, which allowed her to act on her new ideas.

Energy Work and Help from the Other Side

An important factor in managing your Internal Rule Book is to clear your energy field so that you can become a better conduit for what your Soul is trying to tell you. This helps you to hear the words of your Soul through your Chatter Mind noise.

We all have an energy field. This is called our aura, which is like a bubble around our body. It flows in and out and around us according to our physical, mental, spiritual, and emotional states. Awareness of the level of your energy/aura is important. The level of our energy/aura colors our appreciation of an event. The Internal Rule Book defines what our emotional reaction will be, but our energy level can help us modify negative emotions.

On one hand, doing a hard workout or struggling with a difficult school or work project can leave us physically exhausted and feeling lost in the question, "Who am I?" or being rejected in any way can send our energy plummeting.

On the other hand, a physically stimulating workout can make us feel great, and solving a difficult problem can boost our energy. Receiving a compliment can make our day, filling us with beautiful energy, and a moment of grace watching a glorious sunrise can fill us with lots of vitality to face a promising day. Our baseline energy can make a difference. I always give my clients energy at the beginning of a session to lift their vibration. Lifting our vibration not only can help us enhance our ability to communicate with spirits, it also can put us in a good mood.

People around us give and take our energy. There are those people who we love to be with, and when we leave them, we are still riding high, full of energy. Spend as much time as you possibly can with these people.

Then there are people who seem to fill us with energy, but when we leave them, we're exhausted. Basically, your energy field met and joined with the other person's energy field. What a great high! But when the two of you part, your friend has kept your energy. Ouch! You might want to see if that friendship is based on surreptitious energy sucking or if that was just a onetime occurrence.

Then there are the "complainers" who always complain about the same thing. We feel like we're being helpful when we listen to them, but it can be a very depressing experience, which brings us down. In fact, instead of helping these people, we are just enabling them—and they're taking our energy. Stop enabling them and protect your energy!

Other people can make us cringe just at the thought of them. These are energy thieves. Stay away from them too. Unfortunately they are often relatives, which makes this more difficult to do, but do your best to stay away from them as much as you can.

We use or lose energy and then we replenish ourselves by resting. Young children tend to run around until they collapse. They then sleep some, but pretty soon they're up and running again.

As we grow older we continue this pattern of using energy and then replenishing it. The "refill" is absorbed by our whole body. As we become adults, we become less adept at absorbing energy through our whole body. Our intake becomes more selective. This is because our bodies gradually shut down as we age.

Negativity

Assessing your energy baseline and keeping in mind that aging hinders our automatic replenishment, we need to find ways to refill it. These ways can include various forms of exercise, such as yoga, walking, swimming, and chi gung among others. We also need to be aware of how we can lose energy during the day, which allows negativity to shroud us.

For example, you might wake up one morning and feel great. It's a beautiful day and you're going to make the most of it! You get into your car and drive to the supermarket. Just when you get there, however, someone steals your parking space. *Okay, I'm not going to let that upset me*, you say to yourself. You drive around and find another place to park. You get out of your car, and as you walk to the store's entrance, someone honks loudly because they want you to move. A bit jarred, you continue on.

Once in the store, someone bumps into your cart. Another person blocks the shelves where you need to get something. When you nicely ask them to move, after waiting awhile, the shopper gives you a nasty look and doesn't budge. Then as you finally make your way to the cashier, someone runs in front of you with a full cart and cuts you off, taking your place. Each event is registered in your Internal Rule Book and also triggers an emotion, in this case probably something to do with abuse. Meanwhile your Chatter Mind is having a field day with disparaging comments about you!

What happened to your beautiful day?

Our lower state of energy allows negativity to seep in and grow. Similar to our Internal Rule Book all of our experiences collect in the energy field, or aura, around us. In a sense, as more irritating things continue to happen, it's as though the word *victim* gets etched on our forehead, and we attract more irritating things and people to us as negativity descends on us like a dark rain cloud.

How do we stop this? Fortunately it's easier to clear the aura than the Internal Rule Book. You simply need to cleanse the energy around you by smudging yourself. *Smudging* is the term for clearing someone's energy field or any space using sage or incense. It's like taking an eraser and erasing the word *victim* from your forehead. It also lifts a good bit of negativity.

Smudging with Sage

Here is how to clear your energy field by burning sage. I prefer to use sage from South Dakota instead of white sage because I can give it instructions. I can burn it to clear negativity, use it as a medicinal tea, or add it to food I'm cooking with the intention of bringing healing.

To conduct a smudging ceremony you need sage, something in which to burn the sage, and a lighter. Because of my training in First Nation ceremonies, I know the importance of the four elements—earth, water, fire, and air—in sage smudging. Earth is represented by the sage, water is represented by an abalone shell, fire is represented by the burning of the sage, and air is represented by the smoke.

Begin with a prayer with your intention. Are you clearing space around you alone or with a group? Are you clearing a room or an apartment? An office or house? Why? Rather than use a tied up bundle, I prefer to use pieces of sage because it's easier to control how much I'm burning. Carefully light the bundle of sage and gently move the smoking container up and down around yourself or the person or space you are smudging. Feel free to add more sage and relight as needed.

A word of caution: If you do use a smudging bundle it can be a bit tricky. A very, very long time ago, someone gifted me with a smudging bundle, which was almost a foot long and loosely bound. In the springtime I enthusiastically decided to clear my house of all negativity. I lit one end of the bundle, and I proceeded to walk around my house waving it. As I walked around, the bundle began to burn more quickly so, wanting to finish up more quickly, I walked faster. This only created more smoke and lit the bundle up in flames. By this time I was upstairs with an out-of-control smudge bundle that I threw in the bathtub and finally smothered with water, only burning the rug in the bathroom slightly.

The smoke alarm went off, and the excellent system I had wired to the fire department worked quickly, as I immediately heard not only the deafening noise of my house smoke alarm but also the loud siren of the fire truck that was stopping in front of my house.

The kind fireman smiled as I calmly answered the door, very embarrassed. He asked if the fire had started in the kitchen. Just as I was mumbling something like "Oh, kitchen, ah, right," another fireman walked in holding the half-burned smudge bundle, which I had tried to hide behind the garbage cans out back. Busted! The firemen had a good laugh as I explained what I had just tried to do. They didn't need to tell me not to do that again.

So a word to the wise! Be careful with smudge bundles. They can be dangerous. It's very hard to make a good smudge bundle. It needs to be tight enough that it doesn't immediately all catch on fire, but loose enough to burn on its own and not need constant relighting. It is also important to ensure that the smudge bundle was made with a great deal of prayer and good intention.

Good, Good, Good Vibrations

The Beach Boys had it right when they sang about good vibrations. They were probably referring to the invisible sensations that we feel. We really do carry vibrations that are slower when we are depressed or angry and higher when we are happy or in love. Understanding this, it makes sense that music can have a significant effect on us. Music is a source of vibration that we consider either pleasing or exciting, or depressing or irritating. In other words, we attribute a value judgment to the vibration. This value judgment depends on our life experiences from a fetus onward. There are sounds the infant can hear in utero that will affect their whole life. For example, sounds or music heard in utero that help an infant calm down and go to sleep may do the same for the baby after it is born and for the adult that baby becomes.

Vibrations around us make a huge difference not only to our mood but also to our health. As stated previously, while we may believe that our body ends with our skin, in reality we are surrounded by an aura of energy. Depending on the level of energy we harbor, the aura can be large or small, but it always exists and, because this energy goes through our bodies, vibrations can greatly affect us emotionally and physically as well.

Different frequencies can actually penetrate our body and affect certain organs. Radiation therapy sends a high frequency vibration into a specific area. The vocal toner Shulamit Elson is well versed in finding a specific tone to heal different areas of a client's body. Tibetan singing bowls effectuate healing on people simply by placing the bowl on the afflicted area of the body and playing it.

In my work, raising the client's vibration is key to a good session. This goes hand in hand with raising their energy level. The higher vibration helps to cleanse a negative cellular memory allowing someone to free themselves from emotional or physical pain.

Special Helper Spirits

Contacting spirits demands a fairly high vibration. It seems that the higher vibration a person has, the better their potential is to converse with the spirit world. In my book *Seeing the Dead, Talking with Spirits* I describe how I met my spirit guide Tatonka. He is a Lakota medicine man who first saw me when I was about five years old. He decided to join me because I was sickly and needed his help. I think in the Incarnation Planning Time it was planned that he would join me. Not only has he helped me out of some hard situations, he's enabled me to communicate with spirits and feel comfortable and protected as I do so. His influence on me initiated my interest in Lakota ceremony.

As I opened up to my gifts of mediumship and energy healing, I needed to be more grounded. I'm a "flight risk," meaning that it's easy for me to communicate with spirits and not be as aware of incarnate or physical life. Participating in Native American ceremony helps me to stay open to spiritual communication while I remain very much involved in all aspects of physical life.

While keeping us in touch with Mother Earth during the preparations, these ceremonies also take us out of our physical bodies. In this way we gain perspective on our lives, and we can even see the cage that our Internal Rule Book has put us in. All this happens while still being firmly in our physical body.

Opening in this way allows us to bypass the Chatter Mind. It also allows us to enjoy better communication with our own Soul and not only our birth guide but also other spirits who have come to help us. In the context of a sacred ceremony where the area is first smudged and thus cleansed, there is no worry that some negative spirits might bother us. In fact, if we have some unpleasant spirits around, we can remove them during a sacred ceremony.

There are all kinds of ceremonies that can be conducted. They range from being a private daily connection to the Creator and Mother Earth to being present with a gathering of a few or many people. One example is the sweat lodge ceremony. The basic intention of this ceremony is purification of mind and body. It is a wonderful opportunity for the physical body and the Soul to meet, unite in prayer, and create coherence. Often before the ceremony begins prayer ties are made where each participant puts their prayers into a small amount of tobacco wrapped in squares of fabric. These are taken into the sweat lodge and draped above the participant's head. During the ceremony drumming and singing invite helpful spirits in. They read the prayer ties and work with the individual participants. This can be a very emotional and challenging experience as old beliefs and invisible fences are removed and a new perspective appears.

During the ceremony, everyone sits around the perimeter of the sweat lodge, and hot rocks in the middle are showered with water, which creates a great deal of heat, testing the physical body. Just remaining in that oppressive heat can be daunting. Depending on the nature of the prayers the whole experience can seem more difficult. If someone is dealing with a dramatic issue such as loss of love or a job, or illness and fear of death, as the sweat lodge heats up, the burden of that issue becomes so heavy that the participant is forced to release it. That release is essential. It is at that moment when participants feel they can no longer stand the heat that they release the burden and open up to a higher power and really connect with their Soul. That's when spirits can remove heavy burdens and bring in a new perspective that we might call inspiration. When we leave the sweat lodge our physical body has freed itself of toxins through sweating, and our spiritual self has opened the gate to a new perspective and opportunities.

I need to mention that all sweat lodge ceremonies are not alike. It is very important to know what kind of lodge it is as well as the background and training of the leader of the ceremony. Another note is to let the leader of the ceremony know about any medical issues you might have. However, done properly, sweat lodges are very safe and healing for everyone, regardless of age. In my sweat lodge ceremonies, I have had participants from 9 months old to 82 years old, and every age in between.

Raquel's Baby

Raquel wanted a baby very much. She was forty and had had several miscarriages. Her husband was supportive of their efforts, but Raquel was beginning to lose hope. Raquel's prayer as she entered the sweat lodge before the ceremony was, "Please let me give birth to a healthy baby." A couple of months later Raquel conceived, but this time she managed to carry the fetus through birth and beyond. Raquel was so pleased and grateful for her success that one day, as the participants for a ceremony were lining up to go inside the sweat lodge, Raquel sat there proudly with her beautiful baby boy telling everyone, "If you don't believe in the power of the sweat lodge, I have living proof that it works."

Virtual Ceremonies

While a gathering is usually done in person, it's possible to have a virtual gathering as well because spirits can work through the internet and energy is magical. When we were no longer able to conduct our monthly sweat lodge ceremony due to COVID-19, I initiated a weekly virtual prayer and pipe ceremony. This is a prayer gathering for people who carry the sacred pipe or canupa, and for people who want to pray. Since March 2020 we have been meeting virtually every Saturday at noon, focusing our prayers on one of the four cardinal directions. There are participants from across Turtle Island. Participants from South America and Europe were there as well. I was able to see the spirit helpers of all the participants. It was a powerful and uplifting gathering. Many new spirits would gather with us when the ceremonies were taking place. Many prayers were answered thanks to those gatherings. As I am writing this book, I am still leading our weekly virtual prayer and pipe ceremony every Saturday at noon EST. I am also leading sweat lodge ceremonies monthly.

Healing Spirits

Reiki is a Japanese form of energy healing used to encourage emotional or physical healing. People who study Reiki begin by learning certain symbols. These symbols call in healing spirits who work with the practitioner to create wellness. The spirits join the practitioner for the duration of the healing and when it's over, they leave.

The Holy Spirit, Jesus, Mary, and Mary Magdalene are also spirits who can appear to facilitate a person's healing. Usually they will appear for people who are Christian, but they are not exclusive to Christians. There are other spirits from different religions, such as Mohammed, Abraham, Moses, and many others, who can appear when an energy healing is taking place. For the most part these spirits are not visible to people; however, people often sense their presence. Mary and Mary Magdalene also bring a delicious scent of roses when they are helping out. People who are more clairvoyant or clairaudient will see and/or hear them. In my practice I have seen and felt the presence of all of them at different times when I have been doing energy work with a client. The client's personal religious belief or lack of does not necessarily correlate to the spirit who shows up to help. This indicates to me that healing energy is universal and comes from a higher benevolent source.

7

Past Lives, Then and Now

IT'S VERY HELPFUL TO UNDERSTAND that the roots of our current behavior lie in our past, which can include our past lives. One's Soul has culled hundreds of past lives to help it set goals and draw on personality traits to impose on a physical body in its present incarnation. At the same time our physical body has its own history of past lives that it has experienced and transferred through DNA to a present-day incarnated body.

All of our past-life events are easily accessible by our Soul. But because it's not in our physical body's conscious inventory, it's not so easily accessed by our conscious mind. It's also the case that our physical body can't distinguish between past-life or current life entries into our Internal Rule Book. That means that the impact of being burned at the stake for speaking out in front of a group in a past life holds the same emotional kick as being attacked for speaking out in front of a group in one's current life. The result is fear. Because we often don't remember the past-life event, we can't figure out why we are so terrified of speaking in front of a crowd. Identifying that past life and detaching from it can remove that automatic emotional reaction to speaking in front of a group.

Where Do Past-Life Memories Come From?

A good way to look at past-life memory storage is by comparing it to a modern computer. Someone gives you a computer. Although it has a certain amount of storage, as far as you can tell the computer is empty. You begin storing Internal Rule Book memories or events directly on the computer. However, you can add to that memory storage by storing memories, usually older ones, on the cloud. All of our past lives are stored in a similar way. Let's call it our spiritual cloud. Since we didn't actively store a past-life experience during our present-life incarnation, we don't know that this past-life experience even exists. It is only when we journey to find the point of entry of some uncomfortable behavior that we discover what pertinent past-life material is stored on our spiritual cloud.

Most of our past lives only come to our consciousness when they're triggered by a current event. Very often when I'm helping a client overcome an obstacle in their current incarnation we simply need to visit the childhood origin of a rule in their Internal Rule Book. In the following two cases, however, it was necessary to dig more deeply by delving into a past life that had been triggered by an event in my client's current lifetime.

The Root Cause of Flora's Back Pain

Flora had a constant pain in her back between one of her shoulder blades and her backbone. She had been to many doctors to find the source of this discomfort but none of them could figure out what the cause of this chronic pain could be. Flora came to see me. We discovered that her pain had started about the same time that she'd begun dating a man whom she'd fallen in love with. She couldn't imagine that there might be a connection between her pain and her wonderful boyfriend. But in fact, the pain became intolerable when he proposed and she accepted.

We did some Journey Work that took us to a past life. In that past life Flora had fallen in love with a wonderfully romantic man whom she married. It seemed that everything was fine but the truth was, he preferred men. As Flora began to question his lack of performance in conceiving a child, he began to panic. Homosexuals at that time were punished and killed. One evening Flora's husband sneaked up behind her and stabbed her in the back, and she died. In her current life, Flora's body was trying to protect her from making the same mistake. Flora called off the engagement and her back pain disappeared. A couple years later Flora's fiancé came out as being gay. Flora did meet another man, and this time she didn't experience any back pain. They married and now live happily together.

The Betrayal of Karl

Karl had a mysterious pain in his neck. It seemed to him that the same pain had been with him his whole life. He couldn't remember a time when it wasn't there. The pain wasn't always terrible but it never went away. He had seen many doctors, but like many other similar cases, no one had found a source. I did a journey with Karl, looking for the source of his pain.

Spontaneously Karl described being in a foreign place that he had never been to before. He found himself dressed in unusual clothes, which he described as being similar to clothing worn in ancient Rome. Right away I realized that Karl was visiting a past life. I asked him to explain what was going on. He said he seemed to be having fun with a group of people who appeared to be his friends. They were outside talking and smiling. One individual—Dan—seemed to be a closer friend than the others. At one point, the group disbanded and everyone left, except for Dan.

Night was coming on and it was getting dark, when Karl's friend Dan pointed to something behind Karl. When Karl turned around to look, he felt a horrendous pain in his neck. Turning to look at his friend, Karl realized that Dan had just stabbed him in the neck with a knife. As Karl fell to the ground Dan pulled out the knife and left

Karl to die. I asked Karl if anyone in the group looked familiar. He said the one who was his closest friend Dan looked like a boy he'd known his whole life. He had never really liked him and always felt uncomfortable around him. Being near the boy who had murdered Karl in a past life was enough to trigger that warning pain in Karl's neck.

Once we understood the source of Karl's pain, we were able to clear the connection with that past life and his neck pain disappeared.

Denise's Erroneous Belief

While at university Denise and Jim had dated for a few years. They were in love, and marriage seemed the obvious next step. The only problem was that Jim wanted to have children, and Denise was terrified of giving birth. Denise herself didn't understand this fear. She loved children and on some level wanted to have a family. She loved Jim and thought that he would make a wonderful father. Whenever the conversation came around to having children, though, Denise's reticence created doubt and division between what otherwise was a happy couple.

They were at the point of breaking up when Denise decided to see me. She was in tears as she told me how much she loved Jim and didn't understand why she didn't want to have his baby—or anyone else's for that matter. I suggested doing some Journey Work and Denise agreed.

When we got to the point of discovering the obstacle preventing Denise from wanting to have children, Denise entered a past life. She described to me how she was married in that past life and identified Jim as her husband. The marriage began in joy and the happy prospect of having children together. During the first pregnancy, however, Denise had a very hard time. She gave birth to a sickly baby who died shortly after birth.

When this happened, both she and Jim (in that past life) were devastated. Denise went on to describe how, soon thereafter, too soon *really, she had gotten pregnant again. This pregnancy seemed to go much better and she gave birth to a lovely boy. In that past life she and Jim were delighted with their son, but Denise never fully recovered from the pregnancy. Soon Denise was again pregnant and this time gave birth to a girl. The daughter was not a very healthy baby and Denise, already in rough shape, got worse. The whole situation was miserable for Denise, who had to care for her sick daughter while being ill herself. Rather than improve, everything in that past life got worse. Her son had an accident and died. Denise's husband never recovered from losing his son and fell ill. Denise, not well herself, took care of her husband as best she could. Then her daughter fell ill too. Eventually Denise's daughter, and then her husband, died. She herself survived only long enough to hate being alive.*

How was it that Denise was so vulnerable to that past-life trauma? The Internal Rule Book held the answer. Denise had a truly awful child-hood, with a mentally ill mother and absent father. Often her mother would blame Denise and her two siblings for her misery. Denise's mother would complain the most when one of the children was ill, which caused extra work for her. In addition to Denise's Internal Rule Book being filled with her perceived failures and inadequacies, Denise included the idea that children brought only unhappiness. This triggered her past life where she was happy until she had children, whose illnesses drained all the joy from her life. Of course, this caused Denise to fear marriage and children.

I cleared that horrible past-life memory from Denise and also cleared her childhood memory of equating children to misery and brought her to her present incarnation. This current incarnation was her opportunity to live a happy life with Jim. By the end of the session Denise was optimistic about having children. She and Jim got married and they had a son and a daughter together. Denise's children were healthy and so was Denise. Jim and Denise seemed to have a complete do-over from their past life together.

Barbara and the Pigs

Barbara, in her late fifties, had a dysfunctional marriage. Her husband, Al, was uncaring and dictatorial with her, and even though Barbara knew he had a mistress, she couldn't stand up to him. When Barbara came to see me she wanted to know why she was so impotent when dealing with her husband, whom she now hated.

Barbara and I journeyed to the origins of her problems with her husband. Immediately Barbara started describing a past life where she lived in a small shack on the property of a large estate. As a very young teenager she had been forced to leave her family because they couldn't support her. In her new home, the shack next to the pigsty, her job was to care for the pigs.

In the beginning the lord of the manor seemed kind to her. It wasn't long before he seduced her, bringing her gifts that dazzled her. The lord of the manor lived in his mansion with his wife, who turned out to be barren. The first time Barbara got pregnant, all the pleasure of the lord's visits disappeared as he took her baby and gave it to his wife. After that the lord would come down to the pigsty and rape Barbara, who no longer welcomed his advances. If Barbara complained she was severely beaten.

Every time Barbara got pregnant, the lord of the manor would take away her baby and give it to his wife. Barbara had four or five babies in that past life. Each time she was forced to give the newborn to the lord's wife. Barbara was not allowed to see any of the babies she'd birthed. Instead, she was forced to live quietly with the pigs.

One day when the lord came to visit Barbara she began to bitterly complain about her abuse and the loss of her children. In the past the lord would beat her to such an extent that it would silence her. This time, as he turned to take a stick to beat her, Barbara grabbed a pitchfork and stabbed him in the back. Vividly Barbara described the blood coming out of the holes the pitchfork had made in his body as he fell to the ground. Barbara continued attacking him, and he died. Barbara meticulously chopped up his body, feeding the small pieces of it to the pigs. She buried his bones.

The authorities came by looking for the lord because his horse was found wandering, but Barbara claimed she didn't know anything about it and hadn't seen the man. There were robbers in the area so the authorities believed her, attributing his death to them.

As she was leaving this past life I asked Barbara if anyone in it reminded her of anyone she knew in her current incarnation. Barbara identified the lord of the manor as her husband, Al, in her current life. Al's wife in that past life was his mother in his current life, Barbara's mother-in-law, who made Barbara's life miserable. Al would always give preference for everything to his mother over Barbara.

After leaving that past life and as we were still journeying together, I took Barbara to the event in her current incarnation that had triggered that past-life memory. Barbara went to a time when she was pregnant with her first child. She had been gardening and was tired when her husband, Al, arrived home from work. She asked him to help her finish up. Disdainfully he refused to help her and walked away. When Al turned to leave, Barbara imagined herself grabbing the pitchfork and stabbing him in the back. She especially remembered the blood coming out of the holes the pitchfork had made in his back. It was the same vision she had just seen in her past life. All that blood. Barbara didn't actually stab her husband, but the vision was so real at the time that it startled her. It was the same vision from her past life.

Barbara had another current life trauma when her husband had forced her to have an abortion. They had three children, and Al just decided that was enough. To some people it seems that an abortion can't be forced on an adult woman, but it very well can be through severe bullying and dominance. Barbara, a devout Catholic, never could forgive herself for this. Rather than confirm the villainous nature of her husband, it made her feel totally incompetent and bad about herself.

Looking at her situation it's obvious that Barbara was working out her spiritual relationship with Al. Her attraction to Al was based on the same factors as it had been in that past life. Al was wealthy and had originally tried very hard to seduce Barbara, and she had accepted him gratefully. It was not too long before Al proved to be the arrogant "lord of the manor" that she had known in her past life. Barbara never had any spending money and had to cook and clean endlessly. Her only joy was her children.

Nevertheless, because of her children, Barbara always supported Al and tried to be the perfect wife, although she seemed to constantly fall short. Once that past life was revealed, Barbara's hatred of her husband intensified, to the point that she wanted to leave him. But she couldn't. It seems that the act of murdering him in a past life was a stain on her spiritual path that, coupled with her own personal guilt of having an abortion, prevented her from freeing herself. She stopped her sessions with me and hunkered down to soldier through her personal misery.

Barbara's Soul had remembered her past life to the point of attracting her to Al and then staying with Al regardless of his transgressions. In her present incarnation Barbara was exceedingly gentle. She even spoke with a soft, baby voice. Her Soul managed to fill her Internal Rule Book with many rules about being gentle and allowing her husband to do whatever he wanted whenever he wanted. His word was law. Even though he pushed her to the brink, she would not leave him or show any violence toward him. She was, in this way, punishing herself. This is an example of someone whose Internal Rule Book and Chatter Mind prevented her from escaping her prison. For me personally it's very frustrating when a client sees an escape route but backs away from it. All I can do is offer encouragement, which is accepted or not.

Andrew, the Crab Lover

Andrew, a man of about forty years old, was suffering from horrendous nightmares, which he would awaken from, screaming. In these nightmares he was often drowning. Although Andrew wasn't interested in spirits or spiritual connection, he did want to resolve the problem of his nightmares. We decided to journey to find out where this had all begun. It wasn't obvious that Andrew had anything wrong in his life considering the seemingly tight-knit connection between him and his siblings and his personal business success.

In observing a past life Andrew immediately described himself as a young boy who loved to collect crabs on the beach. His mother had died giving birth to him, and his father, a fisherman, blamed the young boy for her death. He ridiculed the boy for wasting his time collecting crabs. Part of the boy's job was to repair the fishing nets. While doing this he would carefully free the crabs that had gotten caught in them. This would irritate his father who thought the crab liberating was a big waste of time. The father treated his son like a miserable mistake.

During the journey I moved Andrew forward to the next event in that past life. Andrew saw himself as a young man. He still loved crabs, but he was increasingly ridiculed by his father. He wanted to prove to his father that he was a real man now. It was a stormy day, and the fishermen were fearful about heading out to sea. The young man decided to venture out. He would prove to his father, once and for all, that he was a man capable of doing more than the average fisherman. Out at sea, the storm was too much for the young man. His boat capsized and he drowned.

As I brought him out of that past life I asked Andrew if anyone from that past life reminded him of someone in this current incarnation. He said the father in the past life resembled his actual father in this one.

When we continued our journey to the trigger event in Andrew's current incarnation, he saw himself as a young boy in his current life. He was surveying his collection of crab photos. He had this collection to try to emulate his father who had a collection of photos of racing boats. One day Andrew's grandparents, who lived very far away, came to town and brought him a gift of a framed photo of a crab.

Young Andrew didn't like the frame or the ugly crab photo they brought and must have demonstrated his dislike. His father was livid. How could Andrew be so bad and embarrass him in front of his parents?

This incident triggered in Andrew's Soul the past-life memory of a father who'd never loved his son, a father who didn't understand his son and never had a good word for him. Andrew began to feel that way about his father. His mind began to identify the many ways that his father had shown dislike of him.

A wedge grew between Andrew and his father. The idea was planted in Andrew's mind that his father had never loved him and had always blamed him for everything. The fact that Andrew had started collecting the crab photos to emulate his father's boat photo collection, and rather than please his father, it had gotten him in trouble, confirmed the belief that trying to please his father would only lead to Andrew's demise. The discord between Andrew and his father continued to grow.

Once Andrew understood the negative perspective from which he was experiencing his father, he could begin to seek out moments when his father had tried to show him love and support. This had a positive effect on his relationship with his father, as well as helping with his nightmares. Clearly, for this incarnation, one of the goals of Andrew's Soul, as well as his father's, was to repair their relationship and learn to love and respect each other.

The exploration of past lives can often reveal astonishing back-stories that may be influencing events today. Delving into those past lives with a trained professional can, as we have seen, help to alleviate the strictures of the Internal Rule Book, which were meant to help us even though they frequently seem to create more walls than bridges. Combined with the Chatter Mind, it's often hard to escape feeling dominated by external forces.

8

The Power of Prayer

PRAYER IS A POSITIVE TRANSFER OF ENERGY and an invitation for spirit guides to help out, and as we discussed in chapter 6, everyone needs energy to be able to function; the more energy transferred, the better. Many people ask whether prayer really makes a difference in difficult situations, and from my experience I can tell them that yes, it absolutely does! The only reason we doubt that prayer makes a difference is because we are expecting a specific result for our prayer investment within a specific time frame, and when things don't turn out as we want, we believe that our prayers are ineffective or worse, aren't even heard. Sometimes people believe that their prayers are either too big or too small to be answered.

The reality is that there is a much greater wisdom to life that is beyond our ability to understand. No prayer is too big or too small. It could be that passing a test is integral to someone's future and that extra push of prayer and support of energy can do the trick, or perhaps the timing isn't quite right for someone to pass that test. A client of mine sat for the bar exam three times before she passed. Each time she had lots of people praying for her. In another example we might pray for someone to come out of a coma, and when the afflicted individual doesn't respond, we feel that our prayers are not answered and are perhaps even ignored, especially if the comatose person dies. What is really going on is that the comatose person and everyone who comes into contact with them in any way, including a person praying, are going through a major learning experience. It's devastating but necessary for the mental, physical, spiritual, emotional, and social healing of all those people involved. Even people who randomly read or hear about the situation of the afflicted individual are touched by it to some extent.

Prayers are always heard and answered. The problem for us is that our definition of *being answered* doesn't always match the greater wisdom of life that we only have access to in bits and pieces. We are invited to not only trust in prayer but also trust that the outcome of prayer, whether it coincides with what we think we want or not, is actually the best for any given situation. It could be that the hopeful law student takes three tries to pass the bar exam because she has children at home who need her supervision for another few years. For the comatose patient who dies, this could be their final exit point and their condition is giving them and others time to adjust to their transition.

How We Heal

When we are in a situation of dis-ease, our Soul and the spirits around us can be helpful in identifying the origin of the dis-ease and then bring guidance as to how the resulting disease should be treated. When I work with a client, I am completely open to spiritual guidance to say the right words and allow the correct energy flow for healing. In this way we can eliminate the dis-ease and facilitate the healing of the disease. Sometimes the healing involves life changes. These can be small changes that are easy to integrate in our life such as changing the decorations inside your home, getting a new hairdo or new wardrobe, and reaching out to new friends. More significant changes could be moving or changing jobs or spouses.

Dr. Bernie Siegel, author of *Love, Medicine and Miracles*, wrote about Exceptional Cancer Patients (ECaP). These are patients who are ready to do what it takes to get healthy against all odds. In his book he talks about a cancer patient in her forties who had a lot of trouble taking care of herself. Bernie recommended that she take an hour walk every day at 5:00 p.m. The woman was horrified at this request and couldn't do it because she said she needed to prepare dinner for her very large family at that time. Needless to say she didn't do well. Another patient who responded to the same suggestion fared much better. The self-care component that was needed for healing made the difference.

Let me make it clear that healing can come in many ways and from many people. Doctors and the medical establishment are key to identifying the physical problems a patient is experiencing. Medicine has developed alongside humanity with people learning that certain plants and herbs have specific effects on the human body. Take Senokot for example. This comes from the senna plant that has a laxative effect. Healers were recommending it for that purpose long before it was boxed and sold at a pharmacy. Considering the influence of the Internal Rule Book on the physical well-being of an individual, it's understandable that not addressing those problems could create a situation where the complete healing of an individual is hampered. It's important for the Soul and a person's Internal Rule Book to be incorporated within a regimen of allopathic medicine for complete healing.

Take for example, Drake, who had chronic GI problems. Drake would return to the doctor year after year to try different solutions for his problem. Every visit, he remained positive and did feel better for many months before he succumbed once again to the same pain. Drake came to me to research the issue. I discovered that his problems usually flared up around spring. With more research it turned out that Drake's great love, Blanche, had committed suicide in April, five years prior. Drake felt guilty about her suicide because he believed he should have been able to help her. Once Drake could process Blanche's death, and recognize that he could not have prevented it, he returned to see his medical doctor. This time the doctor's intervention worked permanently.

Prayer in Action

A few years ago I was camping out and kayaking on the Delaware River in upstate New York. I noticed some kind of a skin problem on my upper arm. It didn't look like an ordinary rash, which led me to believe it was an infection. When it grew worse and worse, I went back home and to the emergency room. The doctor confirmed that it was an infection and gave me some antibiotic ointment to put on it.

This was Labor Day weekend, and unfortunately, the infection got worse and the infected area grew. I went to my local urgent care doctor. He looked at it and told me it was a Methicillin-resistant Staphylococcus aureus (MRSA) infection caused by a type of staph bacteria that's become resistant to many of the antibiotics customarily used to treat ordinary staph infections. It is extremely contagious and can be spread to other people through skin-to-skin contact. At this point I began to pray like mad and sent healing energy to my arm.

The doctor prescribed extremely heavy antibiotics and told me to wrap up the area and warn people who I came in contact with that they might get it. I was horrified to have it but felt even worse to think that I was contagious. The doctor told me to see a dermatologist in a week. Well, I didn't wait. The next day I called my dermatologist for an emergency appointment, letting the receptionist know what I had.

On my arrival to the office, even though I had my arm wrapped up, I was treated like a leper.

The dermatologist walked into my examination room covered head to toe with protective gear. She unwrapped my arm and looked at it for an instant before announcing, "This is a plant allergy." I was overjoyed! Immediately I chalked it up to two bad diagnoses by the two doctors I'd seen. They'd gotten it wrong! I got the appropriate medicine for the plant allergy and, as my dermatologist had warned me, it took a long time to go away. But eventually it was gone! On reflection I began to remember all the prayers and healing energy I and others had put into my arm. Perhaps initially I really did have MRSA, which had been reduced to being a small plant allergy thanks to the healing energy and prayers I had instigated on my own behalf.

Prayer Improves a Medical Condition

Sven had been working out in the yard. It was springtime and there was a lot to be done. He was often exhausted but frequently continued to work nonetheless. He constantly incurred nicks and small cuts that he didn't address with the care they needed. One day Sven's foot got swollen and was terribly painful. His blood pressure went sky high. He limped his way to an urgent care facility. The doctor there told him he had a bad infection and that he should go directly to the emergency room, which Sven did.

At the emergency room the doctor conferred with other doctors, and they put Sven on IV antibiotics and other medications to deal with his blood pressure. Sven, already feeling better, was ready to leave the hospital the next day. The doctors didn't feel he had improved enough to be released, however. The following day a nurse looked at Sven's foot and said that it looked a lot like gout. Eventually the doctors prescribed gout medication. Sven was released and continued to improve at home.

This seems like a simple case of misdiagnosis. Or was it? As soon as Sven was in the hospital he had asked several people to pray for him and send healing energy for his recovery. I was one of them. Could it be that Sven had initially had a life-threatening infection, which morphed into gout thanks to our prayers?

Dolly's Story

We were in Alsace, France, attending the wedding of my brother-in-law. Finally, after a year of grieving the sudden death of another brother-in-law, the family could gather for a happy occasion.

Following the reception, a few of us went to my mother-in-law's house where we were staying. It was good to see her smile for the first time in ages. With us was Fabienne, whose husband, Vincent, had died fifteen years earlier after a long, painful illness.

Everyone was feeling good and happy as we dispersed to settle into our rooms. Suddenly, I heard Fabienne screaming hysterically. When I arrived in the living room I found her seated in an armchair with her miniature poodle Dolly lying across her lap. Dolly wasn't moving or breathing. She was dead. Fabienne especially adored Dolly because she had come into her life when she'd been married to her husband, Vincent, before he died. Dolly reminded Fabienne of the smiles Vincent would muster through his painful illness. And now Dolly, too, was dead.

As Fabienne sobbed, she explained that this old, sick, almost completely blind dog had wandered out the kitchen door onto the landing and then had somehow slipped through the railing, falling about fifteen feet onto cement stairs leading into the basement. Dolly was dead.

I stood in front of Fabienne and I spread my arms out.

I prayed to the Creator to have mercy on this family who had suffered so much loss. I stated that this poor family had experienced some joy at the wedding, but it would be wiped out with the death of Dolly. I prayed that Dolly's death could be delayed so the family could enjoy the celebration of the wedding.

Dolly began to breathe. This old, blind, sick, "dead" sixteen-year-old dog began to breathe! Fabienne screamed out that she was breathing! Immediately we drove her to the local vet who already knew Dolly well because of her frequent appointments due to her bad health. When the vet examined Dolly she found nothing wrong. Not even a broken bone. This old, blind, sick, fragile dog had fallen fifteen feet onto cement stairs and was fine. It was a miracle. A resuscitation by the Creator.

Dolly lived on for a few more months and then quietly passed.

Anything Is Possible with Love and Prayer

I was scheduled for eye surgery. The surgeon needed to empty out the liquid and clean out the inside of my eye. Needless to say I wasn't too enthusiastic about that. My daughter Tania had invited me to join her and her family for a month's vacation in France. Three weeks of the vacation was in a house with a pool on the French Riviera. I wasn't going to miss that trip so I postponed my surgery.

The trip was great! I loved being with my three very young grandchildren and Tania and her husband. Every day was like a miracle day filled with much activity, sun, and joy. When I returned home I had to face my eye surgery. I went in to have a final examination of my eye prior the surgery. After all the technical photos were taken of my inner eye, I waited for the surgeon to appear to give me my final instructions. I felt like a lamb going to the slaughter.

I chided myself for not keeping up with eye exercises and practices that I was supposed to do prior to the surgery. I had been too busy in France. I fervently prayed for mercy and that my eye could miraculously be healed. My surgeon came in, reviewed the photos, and announced that my condition had improved and that there was no reason for the surgery. Hallelujah! I'm sure the power of the love that surrounded me when I was vacationing with Tania and her family along with my fervent prayers for mercy had healed my eye.

Prayer Prevails

Jimmy's parents brought him to see me when he was two and a half years old. He had just been diagnosed with a mitochondrial disease. Mitochondria are organelles whose job it is to generate energy, which is then used by the cell. Another phrase for this is cellular respiration, *which is a process by which ATP, a nucleotide that supplies energy for biochemical cellular processes, is produced. For this reason, mitochondria are known as "the powerhouses of the cell." Cellular respiration is the way our bodies convert food energy to ATP; however, if the mitochondria are damaged, this process of conversion is impaired and* as a result, one's muscles and tissues may not receive the energy they need on a regular basis.

Jimmy's parents were told he had six months to live. I immediately began praying for him, and I worked to give him a maximum amount of energy. Serendipitously, Rosalyn Bruyere, the noted energy healer who taught me almost everything I know, was holding a workshop nearby. I went to the workshop and participated in a prayer group that she was leading, during which she asked us to pray using the First Nation Medicine Wheel. She asked the assembled group to name someone we could all pray for. I quickly requested prayers for Jimmy. Rosalyn led our group prayer, focusing on a request that Jimmy's DNA be changed a little bit to allow him to survive the illness that had befallen him.

The experience felt very profound. At the time I remember being tremendously moved by it. Jimmy continued to see doctors and was monitored constantly. His parents, other family members, and friends prayed for him continuously. Eventually a round of tests came back indicating that things looked different and that Jimmy's prognosis was more positive. In fact, as of the writing of this book, Jimmy just celebrated his eighteenth birthday. Was it energy healing and prayers that made a difference? I think so!

Lost in a Free Fall

In our pinball machine adventure of life, change is inevitable and can be shocking. It's fair to say that everyone gets the rug pulled out from under them at some point in their life at least once. Often we are warned about this kind of impending reversal, but usually it comes as an unwelcome surprise. I had been leading sweat lodges for a number of years. They grounded me and helped balance my openness to spirit and my physical body.

One day when I was preparing for the sweat lodge ceremony, I stepped out of the shower and the whole room began spinning. I dropped to the floor to try to make the spinning stop. It didn't. Finally I realized that I wasn't going to make it to the sweat lodge ceremony.

I asked my husband to go there to let people know that the ceremony was canceled. Meanwhile I lay as still as possible to mitigate the nausea the spinning caused. Several hours later my husband returned. By that time I couldn't tolerate my condition anymore. I actually hadn't expected him to be gone so long and had been praying for his return. My last memory was trying to get to the car. The next morning I woke up in my own bed. I had a horrendous headache. My older daughter, Tania, was there. She told me that at the emergency room they couldn't find anything wrong with me besides a slight sinus problem. Nevertheless when I tried to stand up to go to the bathroom I couldn't walk on my own.

The following day I went to see my doctor. Someone had to help me walk and drive me there. The doctor walked into the examining room and blanched. He thought I was having a stroke and immediately sent me to get another MRI. I did and that MRI didn't show any signs of a problem either. It took me several months to be able to walk on my own. During those months my world as I knew it fell apart. In my pinball game I had been whacked into a fast free fall. My marriage, my house, all disappeared. Gone in the months following my bizarre vertigo.

In retrospect I believe that I knew that my life would be turned upside down in the near future. I am psychic, right? But I didn't want to accept that information. In fact I subconsciously didn't want to face all that trauma that created the dis-ease that turned into disease, perhaps initially a stroke. When my husband went to tell the sweat lodge group that I couldn't make it, my friends in the group decided to hold a prayer vigil for me. I think that their prayers and love reached me and I understood that I had a wonderful support group to get me through these next awful events in my life. I eventually fully recovered.

A Sweat Lodge Prayer Is Answered

Lisa, who was in her late seventies, spoke to me privately before the sweat lodge ceremony was to start. Her doctor had told her that she had heart trouble and would need surgery. Lisa obviously wasn't thrilled *with this news. The prayer she was bringing into the sweat lodge was "Please let me be healed without surgery." It seemed like a tall order, but anything is possible. All of us in the sweat lodge prayed. The following week Lisa called me to tell me that she had seen her doctor, and he had said she no longer needed surgery.*

"What did you do to get better?" he had demanded.

"Nothing," Lisa had answered sweetly.

As she told me this story she added, "You are my secret weapon."

Darionne Gets Blasted

Darionne was a client of mine who had come to me a couple of times to help her move forward in her life. This time she came feeling desperate. Darionne was under the care of a reputable doctor who had done all the necessary tests before coming to the diagnosis of stage 4 breast cancer. As I said my prayer for her even though there was physical proof of this diagnosis, I still felt that she didn't actually have cancer. Darionne shared with me that lots of her friends were praying for her. That was good news. We began the session. Darionne was lying on a couch, and I was sitting next to her. Usually during a session I talk to my client who responds to me, and we have an interactive verbal meditation experience. Darionne was completely relaxed, and I stretched out my hands in her direction to send energy to her without touching her.

Suddenly I was engulfed in energy passing through me toward Darionne. It was so strong that I couldn't speak or move. It felt like a massive amount of energy was shooting out from my whole body, not just my hands, sending powerful energy to Darionne. After what seemed to be a very long time, the energy blast subsided. When I could speak again, I brought Darionne out of her meditation. She sat up obviously feeling very good. I was exhausted.

Sweetly Darionne said, "That was quite different from your other sessions wasn't it?" All I could do is nod. Darionne left, and I was able to refill myself with energy. I was fine.

At the next visit to her doctor, all the tests showed that she was now cancer free. Darionne had the happy experience of surprising her doctor who couldn't believe her cancer was completely gone. He wanted to present her case at a conference but he thought no one would really believe him. I know that prayer and the energy session healed Darionne.

9

Game Over

WE ALL HAVE ONE FINAL EXPIRATION DATE, which as we have learned, is established prior to our incarnation. This date is flexible by perhaps a couple of weeks or even months, but it is a final exit. The game is over, no matter the age of the person who dies. The time of death is planned during the Soul's time in the Incarnation Planning Time between lives.

This concept can seem confusing because of the NDE phenomenon, a situation where someone is dying and actually goes to the light but then returns to incarnate life. We discussed this in chapter 6 with the case of Michèle Bögli-Mastria, and in chapter 1 with the chronicle of Anita Moorjani. Because life can be so difficult, our Soul factors in Potential Exit Points in our life plan. These are times when we could die. I discussed them briefly in those earlier chapters but would like to elaborate on them here. When we recover from a situation where it really looks like we are dying, as in the case of Anita Moorjani, it means that we have chosen to return to our body to continue following our life plan. As we've learned, each of us typically has a few Potential Exit Points in our lives. Some of them pass without us ever being aware of them. Usually they happen during or before the most difficult times of our life when we are having trouble dealing with the challenges before us. These are different from the accidents or illnesses that occur, as their purpose is to encourage us on the right path. I have experienced both.

My Potential Exit Points

Earlier I wrote about my experience with the world beginning to spin when I stepped out of the shower. I personally consider this a Potential Exit Point where I found the support I would need to face the significant upheaval that would completely disrupt my life.

On an earlier occasion I was in the South of France looking for a venue for my daughter's upcoming wedding. We were in Cannes on the French Riviera. This was a time in my life when I was opening up to my gifts of mediumship and energy healing. Even though the sunny beauty of the Cote d'Azur lured me toward the superficial trappings of glitz and romance, I maintained my connection with my guides and practiced spirit communication at the same time that I was planning my daughter's wedding.

I was walking down a beautiful street in Cannes with my daughter and my husband when my spirit guide told me I would fall down. At that moment in my mind's eye I saw that the pavement was uneven. Immediately my Chatter Mind told me I wouldn't fall down because I had noted the uneven pavement. As I was having that thought I fell down hard on my face. My husband and daughter were surprised that I fell because I seemed to fall in slow motion.

I was a mess. One side of my face was bleeding and swelling up, and I was covered in dirt. Spirit, though, told me I would be okay. I remember that as I was falling, I felt a strong hand holding back my right shoulder, slowing my fall. An X-ray confirmed that I would be fine, but my face swelled up so much that I couldn't wear sunglasses. I kept asking Spirit why this had happened. Spirit told me that I had planned it.

Planned it?

Gradually I began to understand that I had planned this fall to keep me on my spiritual path as a healer/medium. A week later when my husband and I were back home in the States, I began to understand the significance of that fall. I told my husband I could have died from the fall. He told me that I was exaggerating. Just when I was ready to change my mind and agree, I turned on the TV news to a report about a noted diet doctor, Robert Atkins, who had just died after falling in the street and hitting his head. He had been rushed to the hospital for emergency surgery but didn't make it. I realized that a stay in the hospital certainly would have placed me more firmly on my spiritual path if indeed I'd needed a boost in that direction. I looked up and thanked the Creator for my life.

A Final Expiration Date

Arturo is a great healer. He manages to help people with physical issues as well as other problems. Arturo's mother fell ill in Spain, but Arturo was not in a position to go see her there. He felt horrible to be stuck so far away from his beloved mother while she was dying in the hospital. He prayed and did everything he could by sending her healing energy. To everyone's surprise Arturo's mother recovered and not only left the ICU but left the hospital entirely. She was completely healed as she walked out of the hospital. About two weeks later she was crossing the road and was hit by a bus and died. It was her Final Expiration Date. It appears that we can juggle the Final Expiration Date by a short amount of time, but we can't stop it.

When and how we die seems quite random although it is previously planned. Generally we expect someone to be born, grow up to adulthood, get to old age, and then die. Usually the exceptions are based on unexpected illness. Accidents can happen at any age and shake our world. This truth smacked me in the face when my husband of fifty years was walking the dog and got hit by a car and died.

The kicker is that he had received a clean bill of health just prior to his death.

People often want to know when they or someone else will die. I choose not to know and refuse to find out. Usually our spirit guides will give us a heads up, but often it's so esoteric that we ignore it. Many years ago during a sweat lodge ceremony I got an unclear message showing me that my husband would die suddenly. It was so out of the blue and out of sync with my life at that time that I ignored it. Time passed and I forgot that horrid message until it came true. So I was warned many years in advance but couldn't really decipher the message at that time. Anyway it wouldn't have made any difference. It was his Final Expiration Point.

What Happens When We Die?

The procedure of dying is really nothing more than the separation of the Soul from the physical body, bearing in mind that the Soul keeps track of the deceased physical body as shown in Pearl's story. We know that the physical body eventually deteriorates and is transformed into material that is dispersed and mixed with other elements, eventually becoming something or someone else. Meanwhile our Soul is invited to go to the light. The usual procedure is that a nurturing loved one from the current incarnation who has preceded in death the person who has just died appears as a guide to invite the deceased to the beautiful light of the spirit world. Most of the time the Soul recognizes this moment of transition and accepts it.

The transition to the light is positive and leads to a wonderful situation of peace, regardless of the circumstances of the death. I have contacted spirits who have been murdered, and their journey to the light and the peace they experienced there was as beautiful as that of someone who died at an old age with their loving family around them. The process is designed for a release of emotions, making way for joyful peace.

Yaya's Passing

Many years ago when I had just begun to open up to my gifts of spirit communication I "heard" one day that my mother would die soon. She happened to be in really good health at the time so this didn't make much sense to me. I tried to ignore this unhappy news, but I kept "hearing" the message over and over again. Finally, I decided to take it seriously. I told my brothers and my adult children that I had "heard" that Yaya (this is what we called her) would pass soon and that it was important to visit her and clear up any unfinished business.

Because my mother was in such good health everyone tried to laugh it off but found that they couldn't ignore me. Each of us went to see her and had some very significant private time with her.

A little over a year later my mother suddenly had trouble swallowing. There was no medical reason for it, but it was causing her great distress. She checked into a hospital in Ohio where she lived and one day I called her there. When she didn't answer the phone in her room I called the nurses' desk. They sent someone to her room to check on her, only to find out that she had died.

Immediately I got busy calling my brothers and taking care of the business side of death. It was a few hours later when I allowed myself to sit and pray. Right away my mother appeared to me as a young woman, smiling and looking vibrant and beautiful. She had transitioned to the light/spirit world. Her mother had come to get her. She was at peace there with her husband of over fifty years and her mother. It was a great comfort to me to see her.

The Intrinsic Value of a Tragic Murder

Sean was a handsome, intelligent, active, and happy young man. He was very talented in music and art. From the outside looking in, Sean had all the components needed to lead a successful life. On top of that Sean had loving parents and had grown up in a wealthy community. The problem for Sean was his body chemistry, which was imbalanced and as such, was causing Sean all kinds of emotional problems as he matured.

Sean's parents tried to help him. When they took him to a psychiatrist, he was evaluated and diagnosed as bipolar. At this point in his life, Sean always seemed to wind up in trouble. It seemed that other people who were with him when he was doing something he shouldn't be doing wouldn't get in trouble, but he always did. For example if he and his friends decided to do some shoplifting for fun, the friends would leave in time while Sean would stay too long and get caught by the police.

As he increasingly made poor choices, Sean turned to drugs in hopes of controlling himself. However, he ended up in prison. When he was released, he felt he was ready to lead a life free of trouble. Unfortunately, he was still unable to control himself and once again landed in prison. This time he got caught up in some kind of altercation, and he was murdered. He went to the light immediately and was safe. Of course his family was devastated.

In the spirit world, where he reviewed his life, Sean finally understood why he'd always taken that step too far. As he explained it to me when I contacted him in the spirit world, he said he never could tell when he was crossing the line. Now he understood that it was his brain chemistry that didn't allow him to perceive the acceptable limits of behavior. Despite his chemical imbalance, though, he felt he had a good life filled with ample doses of love and joy. When he died, it was his final expiration date.

He realized that part of his life's purpose was to be murdered in prison. This created a tremendous amount of constructive change in the prison system. Sean was very proud of his sacrifice for this greater good. This also brought some solace to his parents for they understood that what happened had been planned from the start. Sean's Soul had chosen Sean's body to inhabit specifically because of his bipolar condition. There was no way his parents could have prevented this from happening.

The Soul Goes to the Light

When someone dies, and their Soul goes to the light, they have a major transformational experience. Somehow taking that journey toward the light allows a person to be cleansed emotionally and to a certain extent physically. The deceased not only leaves behind their body, they also rid themselves of any pain they experienced, physical or emotional. A cleansing takes place that strips the deceased of the emotional components of the Internal Rule Book. They experience a sense of nonjudgmental harmony and peace as the pure Soul of that incarnation.

During their life review they experience an unemotional, clear-eyed view of good and bad choices. Once cleansed they view themselves as around thirty years old, usually an age when they are in their prime. In the story regarding my mother's death, I knew she had gone to the light when she appeared to me as a young woman. I knew she was free of the physical, emotional, and mental burdens of her incarnation. Everyone I have ever contacted who has been to the light is at peace and seems to be able to fill their new situation with everything they have ever wanted.

While most Souls go directly to the light, there are some who do not. Although it seems like the obvious choice is to follow a loved one to a place of bliss, some spirits don't do this.

Lost Souls

For most people, the transition to the light/spirit world is effortless and direct. But a problem arises when the Soul attachment to an incarnation is so strong that it can decide to hold on to an incarnation. While the reasons for this attachment to an incarnation are based on the individual and can vary, there are basically three main reasons. The first one occurs when someone dies unexpectedly and refuses to accept the fact that they are dead. The window to go to the light closes, and the Soul of the deceased is temporarily lost. Take Brian's death for example.

Brian

Brian was a nice young man leading a good life. One night he was driving back from a small party. It had been fun, and Brian had made sure that he didn't drink too much. All of a sudden a car going the opposite direction switched lanes and hit Brian's car hard, head on. Brian died instantly. Rather than going to the light, Brian's Soul went looking for his girlfriend, Shoshana, who lived in a different state. Later on Shoshana would tell people how she knew something weird had happened because Brian had appeared to her at the time of the accident. The people who loved Brian and prayed for him and his well-being facilitated him going to the light a short time later.

The second reason that a deceased person might not want to let go of their incarnation is because they feel they have unfinished business. This could include responsibilities toward family or loved ones or, in the case of a murder, the deceased's need to bring the murderer to justice or simply to get revenge. I will share with you Susannah's and Phyllis's stories to illustrate this point.

Susannah

Susannah came to see me to contact her father, Harvey. There seemed to be a different quality about Harvey; he wasn't at peace as other Souls I had contacted had been. Susannah asked me to ask Harvey how he had died. I explained that Harvey had an accident. Susannah kept asking for more details. Gradually it became obvious to me that Harvey had been murdered. I didn't want to upset Susannah with this awful news, but she kept insisting on more details. Harvey had been on a construction site, and he had fallen down an elevator shaft. Finally I had to tell Susannah that her father had been murdered. I gently told Susannah that Harvey hadn't been alone when this happened, and I finally had to say that Harvey had been pushed down the elevator shaft. Rather than burst into tears Susannah said, "I knew it! And I know who pushed him. I already received this information from a well-known medium, and I just came to see you for confirmation." At this point, knowing that his daughter accepted the truth of his death, Harvey went to the light.

Phyllis

Phyllis disappeared about twenty years ago. She was in her forties and had three children. Her eldest child, Pauline, was a teenager when her mother disappeared, and she had never gotten over it. I met Phyllis's family about ten years after her disappearance. They asked me if she was dead. It was a strange experience for me because she didn't seem to be an easily contactable spirit, so I assumed she was alive. Phyllis had been quite a fun-loving, wild person who drank too much and hung out with wild people. The rumor about her was that she had met a new man and had gone to a big city somewhere with him. Although surprising, this didn't seem impossible, such was her personality.

As the years passed, Phyllis's family had an increasingly harder time accepting that she would have just abandoned them forever. Pauline, especially, believed that foul play was involved, and she got confirmation of this from Prunella, a friend of her mother who, on her death bed, confessed to Phyllis's sister that she had been with Phyllis when she was murdered. Before anyone could record this or have Prunella speak to the police, Prunella died.

Here is what Prunella described: She was in the backseat of a car driven by two men she and Phyllis knew. They had been drinking and decided to invite Phyllis to join their party. Phyllis, an alcoholic, got into the back seat. It all started out well until Phyllis decided she wanted to go home. The men refused to take her there, so Phyllis began screaming. The men warned her to be silent; she refused. They drove to a secluded area and dragged Phyllis out of the car. She continued screaming. Prunella was terrified and hid deep in the back seat of the car, pretending that she had passed out. She heard them beating Phyllis until she stopped yelling. Then they put her into the trunk of the car and drove off. Prunella, terrified in the back seat, remained silent.

When the men stopped the car again and got out, Prunella heard them open the trunk. It sounded like they were removing something from the car and then seemed to walk away with it. When they came back to the car, it sounded to Prunella like they removed heavy tools from the trunk. After a long time, Prunella very carefully peeked out of the window. In the dark she saw the men far away, and she recognized the place.

It was hours that Prunella hid deep in the back seat. Eventually the men returned to the car, drove Prunella home, and "woke her up" there even though Prunella had only been feigning sleep. A few days later Prunella was shocked to learn about Phyllis's disappearance and the rumor that Phyllis had run off with a new man. Prunella realized that Phyllis must be dead, and that she, herself, was witness to the murder. She hid away for years after that. The two men involved were well known in the community as dangerous thugs. It wasn't until Prunella was dying herself that she became fearless and needed to tell the truth. But she refused to talk to the police for fear of reprisals to her family by those two thugs who were still bullying the community.

Prunella did indicate the area where the murderers had disposed of Phyllis's body. She described a huge field with some trees and bushes. It was there that Phyllis's body was chopped up and scattered in shallow graves. Apparently from afar Prunella had seen the men using an ax and other tools to chop up something. Pauline asked me to find the remains of her mother. This time when I went to meet my clients, I could feel Phyllis's Soul near me. As much as she had tried to hide from me before, probably to protect her family, *she now was here to help me. We alerted the police about what we were doing.*

My clients and I went to a large field surrounded by a wooded area. Phyllis explained to me that there had been several fires in this field so that there was just one place where some of her bones could still be found. My clients confirmed that there had been several large fires over this area. Phyllis guided me to the broken-down foundation of a house. All that was left were the cement walls that seemed to have contained a basement. Phyllis led me to a corner of that enclosure, explaining that some of her bones had survived fire because of the depth and the water in the basement. The other shallow graves had been scorched several times. I indicated the area to dig. We found some of Phyllis's bones.

Once her bones were found and her story heard, it seemed that Phyllis was ready to go to the light. With my encouragement she went directly to the light and returned at peace. As sad as she was to discover that her mother had been murdered, Pauline found immense comfort in knowing that her mother hadn't abandoned the family.

The third reason someone may try to remain unnaturally connected to their prior life once they have crossed over is because the life just lived was full of really horrendous decisions that led to cruelty, exploitation, and great harm to others. This individual is afraid of suffering the consequences of their disgusting incarnation. You could call these lost Souls, but they aren't really lost—they are just afraid of the light. It is not only possible but very important to send these Souls to the light, and often I am asked to do just that.

The Spa Spook

I was invited to a spa because the owner felt a very uncomfortable energy there. She couldn't put her finger on it, but it was a darkness that affected her generally cheerful nature. Some of her customers who knew her well also mentioned feeling uncomfortable. When I arrived I knew there was a lost Soul there. You're probably wondering why the lost Soul was in a spa in the first place. The lost Soul was a male energy who had issues with women. He enjoyed being at the spa because some of the treatments were painful.

I always start out by saying the Lord's prayer and making a connection with the Creator. For this "ghost busting" as I call it, I was burning a mixture of sage and cedar. I did one walk-through, smudging the entire premises. Then I asked the owner if she felt that the intruder was gone. She answered no. I also didn't think the space was clear. Because I needed to go around again burning the sage and cedar mixture, I asked the owner whether the smoke alarm might go off. She said that she had already burned so much sage herself that it would have gone off before if it was going to. I once again began walking around with my smoking mixture.

As I approached a cramped area where there were some cupboards, I knew the lost spirit was there. Simultaneously with that thought the smoke alarm went off. There was pandemonium as the owner ran around trying to shut down the alarm. I wasn't deterred and continued smudging that area. Soon I felt a physical lift as the lost Soul went to the light. The noise of the smoke alarm stopped and a beautiful calm came over the spa.

An Angry Spirit Transitions to the Light

Some time ago, I was invited to speak at a gathering at a client's home. The young son of my hostess had died several years prior, and she wanted to learn more about contacting spirits and share this learning experience with her friends.

The group of participants assembled in a very large kitchen/family room. The hostess had set out some cheese and crackers and other snacks for us. The chairs in the room had been set with their backs to the kitchen table. I was standing in front of the group and just as I was explaining how everyone and everything was wonderful and peaceful in the spirit world, there was a huge crash. No one was near the kitchen table but somehow a large knife had fallen from it.

I immediately knew it was a lost Soul. Everyone jumped, but one woman blanched. I explained to the group that this was a spirit saying hello, and turning to the woman who had blanched, I said, "You know who this is," to which she meekly replied, "Yes," and she confirmed that it was her ex-boyfriend Brad. She had broken up with him two weeks prior, and just a week ago Brad had committed suicide. I realized that Brad hadn't really wanted to die but was making a dramatic gesture and instead succeeded in killing himself. Because he really wanted to live. This is an example of being caught in the emotional tsunami of depression. But for Brad, because he really didn't want to die, he resisted and passed up his opportunity to go to the light. It was one of his exit points that he ended up taking.

Now he was stuck, feeling all the pain and misery he had felt when he was alive. When I was describing how wonderful the spirit world was, Brad had thrown the knife onto the floor out of anger because he thought I was saying that everyone was happy when they died, and he definitely was not happy about his situation. I invited everyone assembled to pray for him to go to the light. Everyone felt the lift as his Soul ascended.

Spirits Are Everywhere

When I was almost finished with this book, I invited my older daughter, Tania, to read the manuscript, which was on my computer. When Tania reached the story of the angry spirit, all of a sudden FaceTime spontaneously opened on my computer and then the whole computer shut down. Talk about an angry spirit! This one was trying to get my attention to help him go to the light. Discreetly I did help him go to the light. I turned on my computer again and Tania continued her reading. Tania was impressed by the timing and noted that this is another example of how spirits use the internet to communicate with us.

Hitchhikers

Occasionally a lost Soul who has refused to go to the light attaches to a person. I call this a "hitchhiker." Usually when a person is very sad or ill their vibration is low. These lost Souls are attracted to low vibrations and will hang out with a person who is vulnerable in this way. Contrary to spirit guides and helpers, these lost Souls will bring grim thoughts to their host. It can be like a vine that grows over a tree. In the case of a human being, the negativity of the lost Soul can plunge a person into depression.

Cornelia's Shroud

Cornelia was very sad when she came to see me. There didn't seem to be any real reason for her sadness. I put my hands on Cornelia's shoulders and immediately I started seeing horrible monsters. It was frightening, but I understood what was happening. A hitchhiker was covering her body like a shroud. As I was sending the hitchhiker to the light, I created the thought of a beautiful garden for Cornelia. I didn't suggest this to her verbally, but I mentally thought of the beautiful garden as I channeled energy to her.

"Oh, what a beautiful garden!" Cornelia said with evident happiness. I knew the hitchhiker was gone, and the shroud had been lifted from Cornelia.

Amy's Imposter

Amy was very excited as she told me about her ability to feel a spirit. She knew that the spirit was a man and every time she crossed a certain bridge she felt him. Amy was in her late fifties and recently divorced. She was sad and lonely. Usually when someone shares with me stories about their communication with spirits I congratulate them and encourage them to continue. But this time I had to delicately suggest that Amy leave that spirit alone. I could tell that it was a lost Soul.

A few weeks later I saw Amy again. She was depressed and looked awful. I could tell that the lost Soul was with her. I asked her if she had continued communicating with the male spirit. "Yes," she answered sadly. "Please help me." Together we prayed and sent this lost Soul to the light. After that Amy began to cheer up. I taught her how to bring the light of the Creator into her heart center and radiate it out, which would protect her from lost spirits. I explain how to do this in the exercise below. All these variations of lost Souls can be helped by sending them to the light/spirit world through prayer.

ᏧᎧ Radiate and Be Protected

1. Sit in a relaxed position without crossing your hands or feet.
2. Take a deep breath through your nose and then blow it out through your mouth.
3. Take in another deep breath through your nose and then blow it out through your mouth, closing your eyes as you exhale.
4. One more time take a deep breath through your nose, but this time hold your breath for as long as you can and then blow it out through your mouth. As you do this, feel your whole body relaxing.
5. Continue breathing gently in and out through your nose, and as you are breathing, feel all the muscles of your feet and even your toes completely relax.
6. Then feel all the muscles of your legs completely relax.
7. Continue moving up your body, feeling muscles relax as you go. Feel all the muscles of your torso and internal organs relax, then the muscles in your back, your lower back, your middle back and your upper back, your shoulders, arms, hands, and fingers, your neck, and finally your face, including your scalp and eyelids.
8. Now say a prayer to a benevolent higher power or goodness. It could be a religious prayer or something you make up. I like to say the Lord's Prayer.

9. Then imagine a beautiful bright light above your head. This is the light of the Creator. If you can't imagine it, just pretend it's there. The result is the same.

10. Now just imagine a thread coming down from that beautiful light. It enters the top of your head and brings that light into your heart center. The light above your head doesn't get any smaller, but your heart center begins to fill up with that beautiful light. Soon your heart center is so full of light that it radiates outward. When your heart center is radiating out the light of the Creator, you become like the sun, and nothing negative can get to you.

I do this exercise every day. When I'm radiating out that beautiful light of the creator, I include my family and loved ones in that protective light. It's possible to repeat this more than once a day if need be.

Facets of the Spirit World and Afterlife

Technically the spirit world is made up of all spirits who have and have not incarnated. The *afterlife* refers more specifically to spirits who have incarnated along with their spirit helpers. It's like a subset of the spirit world. When an incarnated Soul detaches from its physical body, it enters this subset of the spirit world where it experiences transformation, life review, etc. When we arrive to the afterlife, we go through a life-review process. This is a very detailed review of all the choices we have made during our life and the intention behind each choice. While there is a value judgment attached to each choice, there is no punishment for a bad choice. Instead, in a future incarnation we will be put in a situation that's similar to the one in which we made the choice so that we may learn why we made the choice we did, and hopefully make a better one this time.

It's also true that we may experience conditions that we imposed on others as another way to understand the laws of karma (that is, what goes around, comes around). For example, if in a previous incarnation we were a man who treated women badly, in our next incarnation we might be a woman who is poorly treated by a man. In this way, that Soul and its human are able to experience both sides of that situation. That's not to say that anyone in a situation where they are suffering should be ignored and left to suffer because they are "paying their karma." In fact it means just the opposite. People who are suffering around us are offering us an opportunity to make a good decision by helping them. If we decide not to help, that's a bad decision.

What Do Previously Incarnated Souls Do All Day?

The spirit world provides previously incarnated souls with whatever makes them happy. For instance, I contacted someone's mother who told me that she had all the ingredients to do the wonderful cooking she loved to do. Her son explained that her passion was cooking, but they were always poor and his mother would have to make do with the few ingredients they had.

Another person's aunt showed me extraordinary flowers that she could now grow. She cheerfully told me that she could plant all of the tropical plants and cool-weather plants in the same garden at the same time, which she of course hadn't been able to do when she was alive. Someone's uncle, who was an artist, told me about the amazing colors he could now access in the afterlife spirit world. He showed them to me, but they were so unusual and incredible that I couldn't begin to describe them.

You're the Same You in Death

In the afterlife we keep our looks, personality, intelligence, and sense of humor, or lack thereof. We don't get smart just because we're dead, although we can understand some of our unfortunate decisions and try to atone for them. We do seem to have a better vantage point from which to get a different perspective on issues that might be troubling a loved one who is incarnate.

When there is a new incarnation for a Soul this new incarnation does not modify the previously incarnated Soul. That Soul remains forever intact in the spirit world. The whole island of the Soul, of which each incarnation is a peninsula, will create a new peninsula by taking aspects of an incarnation and mixing it with aspects of other previously incarnated souls, or peninsulas from the same island. In this way the Soul island has many peninsulas each related to each other as past incarnations. People sometimes wonder if their cherished grandfather might later be reincarnated as their darling son. The original Soul of the grandfather stays intact in the spirit world as a peninsula of the island, but aspects of his personality could be found in the son that is a new peninsula attached to the same Soul island. But the grandfather's personality won't reincarnate intact in the son as the son will have elements from other incarnations of the Soul island that will create a different personality with which to meet this new life's goals and challenges. When we die, our life with its many facets, including our personality, is captured in a kind of video that will exist forever. That is why I can access someone's Soul many years after their death. Even after a Soul reincarnates as someone else, remember that the Soul is an island, and each incarnation is like a peninsula attached to the island. Most people aren't aware of that attachment that brings us information about past lives. That past-life information comes to us through dreams or meditation.

Furthermore, there are Soul groups that reincarnate together through several incarnations where each Soul takes on a different role such as mother, sister, father, best friend, worst enemy, etc. Using the island analogy, each member of a Soul group would be an independent island and the various incarnations would be like peninsulas attached to the island.

One client asked about a late-term miscarriage she had suffered. She wanted to know what had happened to that Soul. In a case like that, the Soul was not ready to incarnate. It was just a practice run. As part of the experience I saw this Soul had grown older, and the spiritual body I saw was of a ten-year-old boy. "Yes, he would have been ten years old," my client told me. It seems that in spirit form he experienced "growing up," which was surely preparing him for a complete incarnation in the future. Possibly with the same mother. They are part of the same Soul Group.

When they're not pursuing their hobbies, Souls spend time watching over incarnate loved ones and trying to help them or make up for past mistakes. This could include giving loved ones pertinent advice, watching them work, or making apologies they were unable or unwilling to make in life. I have noticed all of this and more in the healing work I do.

A Fascination with Dentistry

I remember having a crown put on a tooth. This was shortly after I began to see spirits. As I sat in the dentist's chair for what seemed like an eternity, I decided to see if there were any spirits around. I noticed an older woman standing next to my dentist and peering into my mouth as well. Mentally I asked her who she was. She said she was my dentist's aunt May. When I asked her why she was here, she said she was interested in dentistry. When I could talk to my dentist, I asked him about his aunt May. It turned out that she was his great-aunt May, and he proceeded to tell me all about her.

A Buried Memory

Jane was only eight when her mother died. Forty years later Jane asked me to contact her.

Jane's mother was delighted to tell Jane how she had spent all her time in spirit watching over Jane and making sure she was okay. She showed me an image of young Jane on a swing tied to a tree.

I told Jane about this. "No, I don't remember any swing on any tree. That can't be right," Jane announced firmly. Despite this, I simply continued contacting Jane's mother. I knew that sometimes it takes a while for old memories to return. Four years later Jane wrote to me that she had found a photo of herself and her mother and Jane was sitting on a swing on a tree, just as I had described it.

Getting the Best Advice

Kelly was very attached to her father and missed him terribly when he died. She mourned his death for years and lived an introverted life. Finally she began to be social again and met Jamal, a very nice man who happened to be Black (Kelly was white). They fell in love, and Kelly came to see me to ask her father if he approved of her relationship with Jamal. Kelly's father was a racist, and he did not approve of her choice at all. We don't change our personality, including our prejudices, just because we die.

When I work I always pray to bring joy and the highest level of healing to my clients. This means that if a Soul I'm contacting isn't giving me the best advice for my client, I defer to the Creator's message. In this case that message was a definite approval of Kelly and Jamal's union. I explained the situation to Kelly and she understood. She stayed with Jamal and they are now happily married.

Laverne's Father Transitions

Laverne's childhood was a nightmare. Her mother, Glenda, as a young woman survived a gang rape when she was returning home from work. She wasn't able to get the help she needed to process this trauma. Glenda married Laverne's father, Herbert, because she thought he would protect her. In fact, Herbert was a narcissist and instead of being the strong protective husband she thought he'd be, he was a cold, oppressive tyrant.

Glenda eventually met Daniel who swept her off her feet and introduced her to drugs. Laverne was two at that time. Quickly Glenda divorced Laverne's father and went to live with Daniel, taking Laverne with her. Their life was very social and full of friends who came over to get high. Glenda continued working, leaving Laverne with Daniel when she went to work. When Laverne was six years old, she'd watch cartoons every morning until a certain show ended. This was her signal to go downstairs by herself and wait for the school bus. Daniel would usually be asleep because he worked nights, and he considered Laverne a burden.

One morning the dog and Laverne were playing, and Laverne was laughing. This woke Daniel up and he came into the living room, furious. Blaming Laverne for his interrupted sleep, he slapped his hand over her mouth and threw her in the bathroom and slammed the door. Laverne thought she would die. Glenda was busy and unapproachable for Laverne. There was no way for Laverne to let Glenda know how Daniel was treating her.

Needless to say, Laverne was terrified of Daniel. This made her want to avoid him and she began to spend time with her father, even though he was a cold and remote person. When Laverne was seven years old her narcissistic father raped her. The experience was so horrifying for her that she suppressed it. Relatives sensed that something had happened to Laverne, but believed that any perpetrator would be someone who attended the numerous drug parties that Glenda and Daniel threw.

No one suspected Laverne's father, who went on a campaign to look like the perfect father. He also made a case for how troubled Laverne was because she was living with Glenda. In addition he told various friends and family members that Laverne was a chronic liar.

Then Laverne's father found a girlfriend. This made him leave Laverne not only alone but on her own. Because Laverne's domestic situation with her mother and Daniel continued to be fraught with beatings by both of them, at one point Laverne left her mother's house to go and live with her father since he had a girlfriend now. Her father, however, would leave Laverne alone at home while he traveled with his girlfriend. When this happened, Laverne would escape to go live with her friends.

It wasn't until Laverne was forty years old and in a stable relationship that the horrendous memories of the rape came into her consciousness. Through dreams and unwanted visions she got the sense that her father had been the perpetrator. To her this was unthinkable. Because he supported her financially, she'd come to consider him her savior.

Laverne came to see me to find out who had raped her. When I conduct a healing journey like this I make sure that the individual does not relive the trauma but instead views it abstractly to then gain control and not carry the fear and vulnerability of that horrendous aggression. During the session Laverne observed what had happened in the past.

Suddenly everything made sense as she realized that her father had been the perpetrator and that he had worked hard to cover his tracks by going on a charm offensive and painting a picture of Laverne as a troubled individual and a liar. This clearly wasn't true. In fact, Laverne, in attempts to better herself, had gotten her GED and then a bachelor's degree and finally a master's degree.

Laverne decided to confront her father about the rape. Her discovery that he did it was his worst nightmare come true. He denied that it had ever happened. When Laverne tried to engage the support of her relatives on his side, they all turned against her. Apparently her father's attempt to paint a picture of a problematic Laverne had been successful.

About this time Laverne's father fell ill with cancer. Laverne was devastated by the whole situation. She still loved her father and was willing to forgive him if only he'd admit what he had done. But he couldn't do that. He even refused to allow Laverne to see him before he died.

Following her father's death Laverne came to see me to find comfort. Without trying to contact him, Laverne's father was trying to speak to me. Not sure she wanted to hear from him, I asked him what he wanted to say to her.

"I'm sorry," he said, over and over again, which I then shared with Laverne. It brought her peace to know that he'd finally admitted what he'd done. It wasn't until he was in spirit that he had the courage to try to atone for his crime.

Shelby Learns the Truth

Shelby was hysterical as she sat in the driveway of the New Dawn Foundation where I see my clients. Her tear-streaked face was red and exhausted. Her clothes seemed to be falling off her. She was inconsolable. Shelby didn't know where to turn. I invited her inside, and we began a session. A year ago Shelby's father, Floyd, died in Texas. Since then she had been tormented by his death, and she had come to me to find out the circumstances in which he died.

Following the death of his wife twenty years earlier, Floyd was depressed for a number of years until he met Margaret. She seemed to ignite in him an excitement for life that Floyd had thought would never return. Shelby and her sister Brianna didn't like Margaret, but they were happy to see their father smile again. When Margaret insisted on moving back to her native Texas, the daughters tried to get their father to stay in the New York area, but Floyd didn't want to burden his children, and he wanted to please his wife. Floyd was retired, and although he was diabetic, he was in fairly good health.

It wasn't long before Margaret began limiting Floyd's contact with Shelby and Brianna. Floyd seemed to be unaware of the limited contact. He considered that his daughters in New York were busy with their own lives. And the daughters were busy. As time passed and it became more and more difficult to talk to her father, Shelby became increasingly worried. Whenever she spoke of her concern to Brianna, she was told, "This is his choice." Brianna, who had always been particularly close to her father, felt rejected when Floyd seemed to replace Brianna with Margaret in his life.

On one phone call, as Floyd was quickly hanging up the phone, Shelby heard her father say to someone who had obviously just entered the room, "No, no. I won't do it anymore. I promise." On another occasion Floyd whispered to Shelby, "They don't always treat me very well here." Shelby couldn't afford to go to Texas, and she didn't even know her father's address anyway.

One day Shelby received a call announcing that her father had died. She was beside herself with grief. Immediately she scraped together the money to go to Texas. With the help of a detective Shelby found out that her father had been to Las Vegas two days before his death where he seemed perfectly fine. No one saw Floyd leave Las Vegas. How was it possible that the cleaning lady found him dead on the floor of his home two days later? No autopsy was done, and Floyd was immediately cremated. Everything he owned was signed over to Margaret. His death certificate stated natural causes.

I contacted Floyd in the afterlife to find out what happened to him. Floyd had gone to Las Vegas with Margaret and her brother. While there he had a diabetic issue and went into a coma. Instead of taking him to a hospital, Margaret and her brother put him in a car. The brother drove Floyd to Texas while Margaret remained in Las Vegas. When they arrived home, Margaret's brother left Floyd, still alive, on the floor. Margaret's sister saw Floyd on the floor and was told that Floyd was drunk. Everyone just walked around him. When the cleaning lady came she discovered that Floyd had died. A doctor came and signed the death certificate, indicating natural causes. There was no autopsy and the cremation was done immediately.

Although this information was devastating for Shelby, she did feel at peace finally knowing exactly what happened. It seemed that she had no recourse in accusing Margaret of wrongdoing, as it would be practically impossible to prove. Shelby did find comfort in learning that her father was at peace now, and that he was reunited with his loving wife. Brianna also found comfort in understanding that her father had never abandoned her but was in a situation where he basically became a kind of prisoner and couldn't contact Brianna. Now Floyd was able to communicate with his daughters from the spirit world.

10

The Language of Spirit Communication

FIRST AND FOREMOST IT'S IMPORTANT TO KNOW that everyone already communicates with spirits. When I was in my twenties and five months pregnant, way before I opened up to fully communicating with spirits, I had a dream that I would have a son and that I should name him Tristan. This was before science figured out how to determine a fetus's sex. I told my husband about the dream, and four months later our son Tristan was born. One interesting note here is that the name Tristan is associated with nobility, heroism, and medieval legends, and as it turns out, my son Tristan loves medieval times and has shown both heroism and nobility in his life.

Your dreams are a way of communicating with spirits. By identifying when we have such a communication, we can build on it and learn to be more attentive to it instead of ignoring it. Learning the language of spiritual communication is the key to navigating through the pinball machine of life. It's the Rosetta Stone for understanding our incarnation and our life experience. It's through spirit communication that we get closer to understanding our Soul, and we gain perspective on our physical body and the baggage that we came in with and continue to accumulate as we mature. Communicating with our Soul is important to our well-being. It's essential to escaping our Internal Rule Book and Chatter Mind and helping us live an easier life and make better decisions.

Seeing all of this through the lens of the spirit allows us to do something about our Internal Rule Book and change some of those unfortunate rules, which alters the quality of messages from our Chatter Mind. We can also gain perspective and inspiration from spirits who not only can help us with what we're trying to do but may also redirect or even save our lives. As well, many people are interested in spirit communication because someone they love has died, and they want to maintain communication with their Soul. There are so many other reasons to be open to spiritual communication, including the fact that spirits can literally bring us joy.

Philip's Little Joke

I was at the New Dawn Foundation, which is my professional base of operations in New Rochelle, New York. It was a busy day for me with many clients to see. That same day the cleaning service was there. When one client left I walked into the kitchen where there was a lot of commotion. The two young women from the cleaning service, who didn't speak English, were all aflutter trying to tell me something I didn't understand.

My next client walked into the kitchen looking for me. Fortunately, she spoke Spanish and explained that the young women had just seen a mouse, which was now in a basket in the pantry. Bravely I walked into the pantry to see a tiny one-inch mouse at the bottom of a three-foot-tall plastic bucket with smooth sides. Deftly I picked the bucket up, holding it as far away from me as I could, to carry it and the tiny mouse outside. Before I could get to the door, however, the mouse came flying out of the deep bucket!

I was so surprised that I screamed and dropped it all. The two young women and my client burst out laughing as they watched the smallest mouse I had ever seen escape. I had to laugh too. When we finally composed ourselves after laughing so hard, my client and I headed up to my office. There I asked her why she'd come to see me. We were still smiling from the mouse event.

"I'd like you to contact my son," she said. "You knew him." It turned out that her son Philip had been friends with my daughter many years ago. I remembered him well. He was a very nice young man with a great smile. What a shock to find out that he had died! To add to the shock, it turned out that he had committed suicide.

As I made contact with Philip, he was very cheerful. He wanted to know if we'd enjoyed the little joke he'd played on us. Ah, yes—the mouse in the pantry. He'd orchestrated that! He knew that my therapeutic session with his mother would be dreadfully sad. He was a kind and generous Soul, and he loved to make people laugh. His mother was comforted to hear from her son and know that he still had his sense of humor.

Philip's joke is an example of the kind of pranks we can play when we're in spirit.

Sing Me a Song

It was a blah morning. I woke up and dragged myself outside to walk my dog, Natasha. There was a gray chill in the air and the weather reflected my mood. My head was filled with to-do lists, and my Chatter Mind was beginning to remind me of what I'd been doing wrong. I was almost at the small park, which had become our sacred spot to stop and connect with the Creator and fill my heart with that joyful light. This seemed like a difficult task that day.

As I drew closer to the park all of a sudden I "heard" the song "Everything's Coming Up Roses," which I hadn't heard in years; it just seemed to pop into my mind. As I focused on trying to remember the lyrics my whole demeanor changed. I took an instant and said my prayer, filling my heart with light and radiating it to all my family members, loved ones, and everyone else too.

Then I quickly looked up the song on my iPhone and listened to Ethel Merman belt out the lyrics. It was as though she was singing the song only to me and for me! I suddenly became enthusiastic about the yet-undiscovered possibilities that lay ahead of me. Gratefully I thanked my spirit guide for again bringing me out of my blahs into an extraordinary celebration of life!

Another day while going for a walk I asked Siri to play "Morning Has Broken" by Cat Stevens. Instead she played "Unstoppable" by Sia. I immediately realized that Spirit was my DJ that morning. Hearing "Unstoppable" was a powerful way to start my morning. After that came some other selections that further enhanced my mood. The music seemed to weave happiness into my morning, which hadn't really started out that way. As I reached the small park where I usually say my morning prayer, Spirit played the "Hallelujah" chorus. It was so appropriate! I'd never thought of playing that myself! The incredible sound filled me with intense joy and power.

As I reached my front door Spirit played "Just a Song Before I Go" by Crosby, Stills, and Nash. Spirit sometimes sends me music during the day or night. One morning as I was just waking up I heard in my mind, "You're the one that I love, oo, oo, oo . . . " I preferred the lyrics that my spirit guide put to this song from Grease, instead of the original "You're the one that I want." Now that's a happy way to wake up: hearing someone say they love you! Just as Spirit told me it loved me, in the following story we see how a deceased man's love for his wife caused him to reach out to her from the other side.

Sandy's Husband Watches over Her

I was preparing myself to go meet Sandy for a session when her husband, Jeremy, appeared. Jeremy had passed about ten years prior. He was happy I was seeing Sandy because he had an important message for her. Because I was in a hurry, I told him that I would ask him about the message when I saw Sandy. Usually sessions with her were full of reports of her activities and her interactions with family, colleagues, and friends. When I had a moment I mentioned that Jeremy had come to see me earlier because he had something important to tell her.

Sandy was delighted. "Jeremy has something important to say to me? What is it?"

I replied, "It's about your car. Have you been experiencing car trouble lately?"

Sandy said, "No, my car is fine, but I did make an appointment to have an oil change done, and I was told that there was a recall about a year ago, which I never dealt with."

"Aha!" I said. "That's it. You must get the recall done right away."

"Well, I did make an appointment for last week," Sandy admitted, "but the recall will take several hours, so I canceled it because I had other appointments. I made another appointment for this Friday."

"Jeremy is concerned that you will again postpone the appointment, and it's very important that you get that work done now."

"It's a really busy time for me right now, but if Jeremy wants me to do it, I won't change the appointment, even though I had been considering postponing it again."

Jeremy had spent a great deal of time with their grandchildren when he was alive and still watched over them. He said that he tried to engage Sandy to help him by removing a photo of the grandchild who needed help off the wall and putting it on the floor. I let Sandy know that he was doing this, and she now knows that whenever a grandchild's photo is off the wall, Jeremy wants her to check on that grandchild.

This is the way spirits help us in our lives. Our loved ones never leave us completely. Yes, their physical absence is excruciating, but their spiritual presence, which can also include physical manifestation, is always there.

Reuniting Emma with Her Family

Olivia loved her sister Emma. They had been best friends their whole lives, which made Emma's death at thirty-one so hard to accept. At the time of her death, Emma was living alone. She had an on-again, off-again boyfriend, Darren, who seemed to make her more miserable than happy. Olivia asked me to contact Emma. When I agreed to do so, Olivia asked if other family members could attend. I agreed that it was fine. I was surprised to see their whole family gather for this session. Everyone seemed very nervous as I contacted Emma. When I did so Emma was happy to see her family and let them know that she was fine. Then her father asked, "How did she die?" The whole family seemed to be holding their breath as Emma told me, and I told them what happened.

Darren had come to visit Emma the night she died. Their relationship had been going downhill, and they seemed to fight all the time. This was taking a toll on Emma, who'd caught a bad sinus infection and was taking medication for it. She had been happy to see Darren when he came to visit that night, but his rationale for doing so was to break up with her permanently. After Darren left Emma felt even more miserable than before. In an attempt to feel better, Emma helped herself to more over-the-counter medication for her sinus infection and drew a warm bath. It was so relaxing in the bathtub that she fell asleep and drowned.

Some members of Emma's family thought that Darren had murdered her. I didn't know it, but when Olivia had contacted me initially, the family had been divided on whether to pursue legal action against Darren or to let it go.

When I contacted Emma, they understood how her death had occurred and realized that Darren wasn't directly responsible for it. The autopsy had shown no foul play. This brought great peace and harmony to the whole family and Emma, too, who had been sorry to see her family upset and so divided.

Learning to Forgive

I had a cairn terrier, Rosco, whom I adored. Chosen for me by my younger daughter while she was in college, Rosco was a symbol of family love and unity. This was especially true when my life turned upside down, and I found myself living alone with Rosco. It was Rosco and me against the world. I hadn't lived alone since I was twenty-one.

One day a neighbor's dog attacked Rosco and, with one bite to his neck, killed him. I was devastated! What made matters worse is that the neighbor lied about what happened and acted about as obnoxious as you can imagine. I was furious in my grief.

A month later, as I was driving somewhere and listening to the radio, there was an interview with a woman whose sister had been murdered randomly by a man who showed absolutely no remorse. This woman forgave the murderer and would visit him to explain to him how much her sister had meant to her. Initially the murderer still showed no remorse. It took years of such visits before he began to understand her pain. Thinking about the pain of losing a sister at the hand of a murderer and how she was able to forgive the murderer helped me to find forgiveness in my heart for the murderer dog and his owner. A few years later I heard that the murderer dog fell ill and had to be euthanized. My first thought was filled with compassion: That must be so difficult for that family. I was surprised by my own reaction. I had really forgiven them. I'm very grateful to my spirit guide who organized for me to hear the radio interview of the woman who forgave her sister's murderer. I learned to forgive.

Receiving Messages to Deliver

In the movie *Ghost Town* Ricky Gervais is a dentist who has a near-death experience. Following this, he is able to see and hear spirits. As soon as the spirits realize that Ricky can see and hear them, they line up to talk to him. This is true of spirits in the spirit world. They spend their time watching us struggle through our incarnation. They try to assist us but are not allowed to interfere in our lives unless we ask them specifically for help.

Because so many people are closed to spirit communication, to them, receiving suggestions from a spirit is equivalent to hearing a foreign language over a loudspeaker. On the other hand, someone who is open to communicating with spirits has lots of spirits trying to get their attention in hopes that their message to someone incarnate will be delivered. In this effort, the spirit will seek out the closest friend of the incarnate person for whom the message is intended.

A Persistent Uncle

A client of mine by the name of Frederica was very good at communicating with spirits, and one day she complained to me that her friend Sivonna's deceased uncle kept trying to talk to her. "Why doesn't he just talk directly to Sivonna?" Frederica wondered. I explained to Frederica that Sivonna probably couldn't hear her uncle and that Frederica was the closest person to Sivonna who could actually hear him. After that Frederica felt more comfortable and shared the messages with her friend. Sivonna, along with her family, loved hearing from her uncle.

When I first opened the veil and was able to see and hear spirits, I saw lots and lots of faces, and I also began to get random messages for friends. This was uncomfortable because I would hear the message over and over until I finally delivered it. Most of the time the message meant nothing to me and everything to the person who received it. Gradually, as I became more comfortable with my abilities, I seemed to no longer receive these random messages, and the faces disappeared too as I learned to control my gift. You will too.

The Bracelet

One night I dreamed of a bracelet studded with beautiful gems of different colors. My first reaction was to keep this gorgeous bracelet for myself. Then I felt that it wasn't mine and that I needed to return it to its rightful owner. As I was admiring the bracelet I noticed a tiny padlock with a key on it. Maybe I could keep this attractive gold lock? But once again I felt it wasn't mine and that I needed to return it.

When I woke up in the morning I had totally forgotten about the dream. It was when I was walking Natasha that I remembered the bracelet. I really saw it again in my mind's eye. I also remembered the lock and key, but this time the lock and key didn't seem to be attractive to me anymore.

I had a Skype session scheduled with my friend Antoine in France at 11:00 a.m. In these chats we would discuss all kinds of spiritual experiences in France, where he lived, and the United States, where I lived.

As we were talking, I remembered my dream. I randomly asked Antoine if he had any idea of what it could mean. To my surprise he answered yes. Antoine had a bracelet studded with multicolored gems that he had in his overnight bag. He and his wife, Marlene, had been caring for a widow named Marie, who lived alone. When she passed away, she'd left the beautiful bracelet, studded with multicolored gems, to Antoine and Marlene—and it was just like the one I'd described.

I realized that Marie had come to me in my dream, identifying herself by the bracelet. The lock and key was for me to know that I needed to research the story of this bracelet. Marie's goal in all this was simply to express her gratitude for everything Antoine and Marlene had done for her and to say hi to them and reassure them that the bracelet was theirs to keep. Why did she come to me? Because I was the closest person to Antoine who could transmit her message to him.

Consuela's Companion

Consuela was preparing to face her first day alone after her beloved husband had died. She missed him terribly! The busy time following his death, with all its details to attend to, had kept her occupied. As well, she'd been surrounded by many loving people who were helping her in this tragic time of transition. But now the last friend was leaving, and Consuela would be alone in the house. The time she dreaded the most was breakfast, for it had been a special time that she'd shared with her husband, one in which they'd plan out their day.

Taking a deep breath Consuela got out of bed to fix her morning coffee. Her heart was heavy as she went through the motions of preparing breakfast. Ever so slowly she placed her breakfast on her side of the table and sat down. Trying to not look at the empty seat in front *of her, Consuela glanced out the window and noticed a new bird at her bird feeder. That bird feeder had been the heart of her conversations with her husband and now it had a new bird in it. A brand-new bird! Consuela intuitively knew it was her husband's spirit coming to say hello. Every morning after that the new bird would appear when Consuela sat down for breakfast. It was her husband having breakfast with her again in the only way that he now could.*

Bottoms Up!

Steve had been the love of Grace's life. They basically lived for each other, creating a bubble universe of happy love. After thirty years, Steve fell ill and died. Grace almost didn't know what to do with herself without Steve by her side. Her best friend, her great love, her everything—was gone!

Working with Grace, I heard Steve suggest that Grace organize a gathering of their friends at a local bar where they all used to meet up. I told Grace to be sure to look for signs of Steve's presence. When I next saw Grace she was dejected and said that nothing unusual had happened, no flickering lights or anything. I asked Grace to describe to me everything that had occurred that evening. Running through a description of the evening and the people there, Grace mentioned how the waitress wasn't great.

"Why?" I wanted to know.

"Well, she brought a drink to the table that nobody ordered, and then she just left it there."

"Bingo!" I said. "That drink was for Steve! It was his way of showing he was participating in the party."

"Of course!" Grace said, smiling. "The drink was for Steve! I hadn't even thought of that!"

Steve also communicated with Grace in other ways. In addition to appearing in her dreams, Steve engaged their cats to help him communicate with his wife. Through me Steve told Grace to buy a helium-filled, heart-shaped balloon for the cats. Grace loved to watch them play with the string and pull the balloon from one room to another.

On the day of Grace and Steve's wedding anniversary, Grace was especially depressed and missing Steve a great deal. She was so depressed that she hadn't managed to get any new heart-shaped helium balloons for the cats. As it turned out, Steve took things into his own hands, or rather the cat's paws. The morning of their anniversary Grace found a deflated heart-shaped balloon somehow attached to the wall next to their wedding photo.

A Congratulatory Hello

When Tatiana gave birth to her second son, Anthony, her many friends sent her emails of congratulations. The most interesting one came from her friend Carol. Although Tatiana hadn't known Carol very well, Carol was such a brave and impressive person that Tatiana always admired her. Carol was born with many body issues. Her wealthy parents were always trying different ways to improve her condition. One memorable way was to break her leg in a couple of places so that it would then grow straight. Through all this Carol always had a smile on her face and was ready to laugh.

Tatiana was delighted to receive this email from Carol, although it was quite unexpected because Carol had died two years earlier. Apparently, Carol's Soul had taken an email she'd sent five years ago at the birth of Tatiana's first son and put it in Tatiana's new email in-box.

Spirit Loves the Internet!

Brenda was feeling sad following her father's death. One day she came home, opened her computer, and set to work. No one was home and she left the computer to get a drink. When she returned HahahahahaHarold was written across her screen. Her deceased father's name was Harold and he was known for his great sense of humor.

The Real Grandpa Mike

One day my grandpa Mike appeared to me unsolicited. I'd always been a bit afraid of him and never would have contacted him. He had ruined my belief in Santa Claus by asking me one Christmas Eve where the gifts were hidden so he could bring them out and put them under the tree. When he registered my look of horror and sadness he mumbled something in embarrassment and walked away.

When I was a teenager he was always criticizing me to my parents because I would walk on the lawn in our small town's square in my bare feet—something that was not uncommon in our college town—and he considered it undignified. Connecting with Grandpa Mike in spirit turned out to be healing for me because I got a new perspective on him. I had always considered him to be a strict military man who couldn't be the least bit cuddly, but what I saw of him in spirit proved to me that he was a good and kind-hearted man. Regarding his admonitions about my having walked barefoot, he told me he'd been trying to teach me how to be a lady. So I guess he did care about me after all. Without the ability to communicate with Grandpa Mike I would have continued to have the wrong idea about who he was at heart.

Patricia Finds Peace

Patricia came to my workshop to communicate with her six-year-old son, Davy, who had died because of medical error. Patricia was devastated and could barely function. More than anything else Patricia wanted to be able to contact Davy. She wanted to see him in her dreams, she wanted to feel him close to her, but nothing seemed to work for her. I could tell that she really did have communication going with Davy, but her grief prevented her from perceiving it. I knew this when she shared that on receiving all the medical records related to Davy's death, only one file reeked of a "medicine smell." It was in that file that Patricia found the papers proving the medical malpractice.

During workshops I can see all the spirits who have come in hopes of being noticed by me and especially the related participants. In this *workshop Patricia shared that one night she woke up screaming. Davy was present in the workshop, and he told me that he had come to visit her that night, but she was so sad that she began screaming.*

After several exercises, I led a meditation where each participant could meet a loved one who had passed. When the meditation ended the participants shared some of their experiences. Patricia looked very happy. She told us how before the meditation began a fly came up to her face and flew back and forth, back and forth and then landed on her knee. During the whole meditation, a good twenty minutes, the fly stayed there. Patricia knew that Davy, not wanting to frighten her again, chose the smallest way to let her know he was around her. Apparently he was quite a jokester, so this fit in with his personality. This experience convinced Patricia to communicate more openly with Davy, which brought her much happiness.

Don't Forget the Animals

Animals engage with spirits around us. In the stories "Patricia Finds Peace" and "Consuela's Companion," a fly and a bird were vehicles the spirits of deceased loved ones used to represent them and bring comfort to Patricia and Consuela. It is important to note that spirits use of all nature's creatures to bring us not only comfort but information. As I mentioned earlier, my dog Natasha is often a vehicle for spirits to show their affection for an incarnate person who feels lonely and sad. She usually sleeps in a corner of my office but will spontaneously get up and approach a client when they need a show of tenderness from a loved one who passed. When that happens my clients always know who is directing Natasha.

A client told me that every time she needed extra help from her grandfather who was a great source of strength for her before he passed, she would see a cardinal. This red bird became the symbol for the whole family. Every time the cardinal appeared they knew that Grandpa was around, helping them out as usual. Another client, Sabrina, was feeling terribly lonely after the passing of her mother.

Before she had died her mother had told her that when Sabrina saw a butterfly, it would be her. Sabrina didn't really believe this until after the death of her mother, when Sabrina was sitting alone crying, a butterfly flew up and sat on her hand. Now Sabrina knows that her mother's spirit isn't far away. It is rewarding for people seeking to feel the presence of loved ones who have passed to look to nature for physical proof that they are around.

In addition to this kind of direct comfort, different creatures can cross our path to bring us messages. In the same way that we can receive messages to give each other, spirits prompt animals, birds, insects, and so forth to show up in front of us to bring us important messages. Yes, even the creepy crawlies that we might not want to run into have messages for us. I like to look up the spiritual meaning of a creature online. Remember that spirits are very proficient at using the internet to convey messages to us. When you look up the spiritual meaning of a creature online the spirits around you will show you a pertinent message for you at that time. Another day when you look up the same creature you might get a slightly different message.

Sue's Discovery

Sue was having a hard time. In her sixties, she had health issues with her digestion that made her diet extremely limited. After having surgery where she almost died, she was very careful about what she ate. This impacted her social life because it was so risky to go to a restaurant. Nevertheless Sue was determined to have a social life that didn't involve food. Then she somehow injured her back. Not really sure how it happened, Sue could barely move without excruciating pain. Bravely she began physical therapy. Then she had a stroke. Fortunately it wasn't a severe stroke, but it did compromise the use of her hands and legs so that she now needed occupational therapy too.

Sue told me that on top of everything else, she now thought she had a roach living in her home. She saw it one day, and it seemed to have come out of nowhere. It then disappeared the same way. I immediately looked up the meaning for "cockroach spirit animal." This is what I found on the Miller's Guide website: "Cockroach spirit animal teaches you to survive and never to give up. To be flexible and readily adaptable in any situations life presents itself with is one of the greatest traits any animal living on this planet could possess." What a powerful message for Sue.

An Unlikely Role Model

Sometimes we are faced with situations where we feel the warrior inside us want to come out and make some noise. I was feeling that way because someone I was working with was acting unfairly. One evening as I was returning home I was plotting my actions. I was in the process of compiling a list of people I would call once I finished reviewing my grievances and how I would present them to all concerned. This actually brought me a bit of pleasure to imagine the power with which I would intervene and change the course of things.

As I approached the entrance of my home, there, hanging upside down from a tree branch, was an opossum. I couldn't help but notice it because it was late fall and there weren't many leaves. Immediately I understood that the opossum was bringing me a message. I looked it up and read that opossums play dead to trick their assailants. I understood; I should take no action and wait. I followed that advice and the person who had been persecuting me got caught up in their own stories and managed to destroy their own credibility. In retrospect I understand how by listening to opossum and not taking action I had avoided making my situation worse. I can just imagine my spirit guide convincing an opossum to wait exposed outside the entrance of my home to bring me this message.

Frequently, when I'm feeling overscheduled, spirit will send a chipmunk across my path to remind me to have fun. Small rabbits also appear and wait for me to notice them. They bring me the message that all is good and abundance is mine. It's quite wonderful to receive these beautiful and uplifting messages from spirit. All kinds of messages that we could miss if we aren't aware of them.

Here's How You Do It:
Seeing the Dead and Talking with Spirits

The most important first step in communicating with spirits is to take that leap of faith and acknowledge that spirits exist. Sensing the presence of a spirit is most people's first experience of spiritual communication. Of course, people may also notice things moving unnaturally and/or see flickering lights and/or hear strange noises, but for the most part they attribute these anomalies to other "physical world" causes. Accepting that these may be spiritual experiences is huge in terms of allowing further communication to transpire. Fear is a great inhibitor. When we feel safe, on the other hand, we are in a better position to open up to a strange new experience.

A little history helps us understand and feel safe. Spirits have been communicating with humans for a very long time. At some point we noticed that people who are dying "see" a loved one who already died and is hovering around them. Usually this brings comfort to the dying person. However, for someone who is not actively dying, "seeing" a deceased loved one indicated that they themselves would die soon. Yikes! This was terrifying. Throughout the years, literature has not been kind to spirits. For the most part they were portrayed as scary and malevolent. Now we know that is not true. Spirits are basically around us to help us. We need to embrace this and leave fear behind. Are you ready to take the leap? If so, read on to learn some techniques to get you started.

Your Best Communication Skill

I regularly offer workshops on spirit communication, and I like to begin them by having my audience name the various ways that we may perceive spirits and the ways they may communicate with us. The following is a partial list of their answers.

External Communication

Seeing spirits with your eyes open (clairvoyance)

Hearing spirit voices or sounds coming from outside your body (clairaudience)

Smelling something or feeling something on your skin, like heat or cold (clairsentience)

Reading and having a meaningful phrase jump out at you

Having conversations with people through whom Spirit may be speaking, thus bringing you pertinent information

Seeing something that makes us think of a friend or loved one who passed

Experiencing coincidences and synchronicities

Strange noises, doors moving, lights blinking, TV on and off, etc.

Witnessing unusual animal behavior at very specific times or simply noticing different birds, animals, bugs, etc.

Listening to the radio, watching TV, or surfing the internet and hearing or reading something that pertains directly to an issue we're having at the time

Hearing music and/or lyrics that seem to directly pertain to something we're thinking about

Internal Communication

Sensing a spirit's presence

Seeing a spirit in our mind's eye

Hearing a spirit voice in our mind

Knowing or intuiting information pertaining to the future that seems to come out of nowhere

Dreaming, both in sleep and daydreaming

Have you experienced any of the above? Which ones? How? Each one of us has their best means of communicating with spirits. Review the list above and see what resonates with you. The most common one is just "knowing." Often people will carry on conversations in their mind with loved ones who passed and get responses. Generally they think they just made up these responses, but that's not true. The responses are really coming from their loved one! Just because the answer isn't in the voice of that person doesn't mean it isn't coming from them. Projecting a specific voice is hard for a spirit to do and can't be heard by everyone. Feeling the presence of a loved one is beautiful. Too often people want to see the spirit but this too is really hard for a spirit to manifest and also requires someone with a higher vibration to see them. I often take my clients on a journey to see a loved one: first building up their energy and vibration, and then taking them to a beach or a garden where they can see and communicate with their loved one who passed.

⌒ꝰ Set Up for Communicating with Spirits

1. In my spirit communication workshops, almost everyone has taken the first step of accepting that spirit communication exists and everyone can experience that communication. Have you?

2. Clear the space around yourself by smudging, which I described in the earlier exercises in this chapter.

3. Sit in a comfortable position. Relax and take three deep breaths, in through your nose and out through your mouth. On the last inhale, hold your breath about thirty seconds and then blow the air out your mouth as you feel your body relaxing completely. Continue breathing through your nose, and every time you exhale imagine your body relaxing more and more.

4. Say a prayer in your mind or out loud. This prayer could be something religious like the Lord's Prayer (my favorite) or some other prayer. Or perhaps it's a prayer to goodness and the idea of a higher benevolent power. After the prayer imagine a beautiful white light above your head. This is the light of the Creator. Even if you fail to "see" the light in your mind's eye, imagining it does the trick.

5. Once the light is strong, imagine a thread coming down from it, entering the top of your head, and then going down through

your head and neck to your heart center. That beautiful light begins to fill your heart center until it starts to radiate out around you. At that point you become like the sun, radiating out light and energy, and nothing negative can get to you. The light above your head doesn't diminish but also remains strong.

6. Establish your intention. Perhaps you want to contact your spirit guide or a loved one who has passed? This meditation is also a good way to better your mind's communication with your Soul. Perhaps the messages you get will be related to your personal life. It's all good.

7. Light a candle. I encourage you to do this meditation with a lit candle because it gives you a focal point. As you are doing this be aware of your thoughts. Don't let your Chatter Mind lead you astray. Every time you realize your Chatter Mind is leading you downhill just say, Stop! Remind yourself of your intention and relax. Be patient. Allow yourself at least 20 minutes to just concentrate on the candle flame. Is the flame changing direction? Is it getting higher or lower? As you concentrate on the flame continue clearing your Chatter Mind, which you can learn to ignore. Draw your attention away from your thoughts back to the flame. What is it that you perceive there? Become aware of sounds and your feelings. Do you smell anything? Mom's perfume? Or hear anything? In this situation nothing is random. Perhaps you might hear your loved one's voice, or simply get a feeling of their presence through warmth or cold. You might get a deep sense of knowing something like the presence of a loved one or something that you just know you must do. Enjoy whatever you receive. As you continue doing this, hopefully on a daily basis, you will receive more results. Don't allow yourself to get discouraged!

8. If you have identified your best way of communicating with spirits, keep that in mind.

If you can't, don't worry. You might be able to in the future. However, if you do identify your best means of communication it's important to accept this and build on it. So often when people are ready to communicate with spirits they have a preconceived idea of how that communication should be. If they believe that communication happens only when one sees or hears a spirit, they might miss a lot of spiritual information coming to them by other means.

9. When you are ready to come out of the meditation, begin by wiggling your fingers and toes. Then gradually stretch and wake up your body.

10. With a word of gratitude, blow out the candle.

11. Stand up, stretch, and feel grateful for the peaceful experience. If you don't think you communicated with any spirits, don't worry. I'm sure you did and it might take time for this communication to get through to you. Be aware of things happening around you as spirits might try to gently show you in other ways that they are around and have messages for you.

Actually seeing spirits is one of the more difficult ways to communicate with them; hearing is more common. Even when a spirit physically appears people often decide they're just imaging it. The same goes for hearing. How many times have you heard a noise somewhere in your house and you attribute it to the cat when it's really a spirit trying to say hello? Flickering lights, doors opening and closing, TV sets turning on or off are all ways that spirits are communicating with us that we might attribute to mechanical error or the wind. Again, the most popular form of spirit communication is knowing, but it's also the most difficult to trust. Remember that practice makes perfect!

You'll Love It

Communicating with spirits is really easy. The more we open up to the possibility, the easier it gets. Spirits are constantly trying to help us if we would just give them a chance. Don't be afraid. Once you begin to identify ways that you are receiving communications, they will get easier and easier to identify.

Once you are communicating with spirits more frequently, and you want to take a break, you can learn to control your contacts. A number of years ago I was alone in a large home with lots of spirits around. My dog, Rosco, was with me. I was exhausted and went to bed, and Rosco came up on the bed with me. All of a sudden he stood up and jumped off the bed and hid underneath it. I was lying on my side, and I heard knocking on the bedside table behind me. Without turning around, I said, "I've had a really busy day, and I'm tired now. I'll talk to you in the morning." The knocking stopped, and the next morning the visitor was gone. We all have that control, so you don't have to worry about spirits bothering you incessantly once you've opened up to that communication.

When I began on this path of spirit communication Melanie Noblit-Gambino set up a spirit as a gatekeeper for me. This is a spirit guide who is specifically dedicated to keeping out spirits and helps me to determine the quality of the spirit I am communicating with. When I'm working with a client I will ask my gatekeeper to open communication with spirits who can be helpful to my client. I recommend that everyone set up a gatekeeper spirit.

❧ How to Set Up a Gatekeeper

1. Identify a spirit guide around you, including the guide's name. You can use the "Set Up for Spirit Communication" meditation exercise above to do this. Just change your intention to communicate with a gatekeeper guide instead of your birth guide.

2. While you are still in that meditation, communicate with that guide and start to develop a relationship with them.

3. Ask that guide to be your gatekeeper. Don't feel bad if the answer is no. You'll just have to find a different guide to take on that job.

4. Once you feel you have a connection and commitment from a spirit guide to be your gatekeeper, trust that guide to do the job well.

Once you include communication with your Soul and spirit guides in your life, the crazy pinball machine ride feels smoother. There's a method to the madness. When you're falling and your life seems to be in shambles, remember that you're just getting an education and better times are always ahead of you. You are never alone, and you always have the safety net of your Soul. Most of all try to enjoy the ride as much as you can because there are always bright lights and good things if you look for them.

EPILOGUE

Conversing with the Spirits

ALTHOUGH SPIRITS ARE CONSTANTLY TRYING to communicate with us, many people wonder why we should bother to pay attention to them. People who've had neither the experience with spirits nor the inclination to pursue a relationship with them may only believe what their five senses tell them. Trying to communicate with a vague something that conveys messages in such an oblique fashion, which could easily be misunderstood, just doesn't seem worth the time and effort.

On the other hand, for people who have opened up to the fact that the spirit world does exist *and* that we can communicate with spirits, there is no question that doing so adds a dimension of comfort to our lives.

For the nonbelievers, I understand you. Your awareness of interest in a spirit world and spiritual communication exists as someone else's fantasy. To me, this awareness could be compared to someone traveling in a foreign country where the people use a different language and alphabet. You aren't planning on living there, so why bother trying to learn anything about that foreign country and its language? However, what you may not realize is that having the ability to understand that language and culture can enhance your life. As well, you're already living in that foreign country, and you have been communicating with spirits your whole life without having learned the language of spiritual communication per se.

First and foremost, you are in communication with your own spirit, your Soul, all the time, whether you know it or not. You are also receiving constant guidance from your own spirit guide(s). Finally, there is a multitude of spirits around you who are relatives who have passed on or other friends and family members who are interested in helping you.

A Greater Consciousness and the Meaning of It All

Is our incarnation a great experiment? Could it be possible that there is a greater consciousness in the universe that maintains some kind of balance that demands that peace reigns? Our body's sole mission on Earth is to show up every day. Our Soul has the agenda of the goals we're supposed to achieve. Achieving those goals brings our body emotionally fulfilling unconditional love.

Throughout my life I have seen how Spirit has helped me and encouraged me on my path. When I was sixteen, I did a lot of babysitting. One evening I babysat a newborn. She was tiny. When she began to cry, I picked her up. Suddenly my whole body was filled with the most extraordinary emotions. I knew that one way or another I had to have a baby in my life. Today I have four beautiful children who are the center of my life. Tania, Tristan, Terence, and Talia have been incredibly supportive on my walk with Spirit. All of them have participated in my workshops and ceremonies. I'm grateful to Spirit for that opportunity to hold the newborn baby so many years ago. It was a preview of coming attractions. That experience anchored my necessity to have children and I was blessed to be able to birth them myself. They have taught me that family is love and love is everything. Implicit in the notion of family is the intention to unconditionally love one person or a group of people. Wonderful, loving families exist, whose members have no biological connections. Our Soul works very hard to help us create our own version of a family. Through this we may experience unconditional love, which, at the end of the day, is what it's all about.

Let It Be

In a "Carpool Karaoke" video with TV host James Corden and Paul McCartney, Paul was visiting his childhood home in Liverpool, England, and he spoke about a significant point in his life. It was late in the Beatles' career, and the group was having problems. Paul was also single and craving a permanent partner. He began to doubt that he was on the right track for his life.

At some point during this time, he had a dream where his mother, Mary, came to him and told him things would be okay and to just "let it be." Those words stuck in his mind, and he turned them into the beautiful song of the same name. Shortly thereafter he met the love of his life, Linda, and the rest, as they say, is history.

In seeking to communicate with Spirits, we enhance our incarnate life experience. Take the first step by practicing the techniques outlined in the pages of this book and then relax, for you've done your part to get started. The spirit realm will respond in turn. Be like Paul McCartney and let it be. Then sit back and see where your path—with the protection of the spirits you've learned to communicate with along the way—will take you.

My pinball machine ride was unique in 2022. In February shortly before my birthday, I took a step outside my door and slipped and broke my wrist on my right hand. Yes, I'm right-handed. Nice birthday present! A few days later I was supposed to fly out to Denver to see my daughter Talia and meet my new grandson Maddox. There was no way that could happen. My broken wrist was really painful, and I couldn't do much with just my left hand. And there was also the question of surgery for my wrist. Taking a flight now was out of the question.

I was very disappointed. Then I realized that this must be a planned event. It was that darn pinball machine of life batting me off in another direction, definitely not of my choosing. I had to take my own advice and use the tools that I have outlined in this book. To start with I fought off my Chatter Mind's unhelpful remarks about how careless I was to slip and fall on the black ice. After all, that night the emergency room was full of other people who had also fallen on the treacherous black ice.

I worked hard to make my Internal Rule Book entry include the positives of my fall. I felt good that I, in the throes of the accident, had the wherewithal to call 911, my son Tristan, and a friend to take care of my dog, Natasha. Living alone, in pain, and not even able to shower or dress myself was depressing, but talking with my spirit guides, I learned what a blessing it was to be able to do anything at all. I developed even more compassion for people with disabilities. My wrist would heal, but some people would never have the use of their extremities.

My guides wouldn't let me miss a beat in my busy life and made sure that I would reach out to others. Independent me had to ask for help. One of my helpers was my husband, Georges, from whom I was separated. I gratefully received his help as well as that of others. My spirit guides wouldn't let me slip into depression. They kept me busy figuring out all the lessons I needed to learn from this event. Another positive is that because I broke my wrist I had time to write this book.

In November, Georges and I traveled from New York to California for the wedding of our son. It was a heaven-made trip full of promise for the future. Our whole family then planned a beautiful trip to the South of France for the following summer. The pinball machine, however, had other ideas. In December Georges got hit by a car and died. Just like that! Talk about a wild year! Because of all the support from family, friends, spirit guides, and my ability to communicate with Georges's spirit, I have made it through these crazy tragedies and celebrations.

Because everything was already set up for our July trip to the South of France, a trip that Georges was supposed to attend, we all decided to go. At our villa there were four lights around the swimming pool. When we arrived, one of them began blinking consistently and continued to blink until we left. Of course it was Georges showing us that he had attended our gathering after all. So it is with the pinball machine of life. It's quite a wild ride! I'm sure there is more to come for me and, with the help of my spirit guides and the spirits around me, I look forward to the celebrations.

I'm so glad I had the chance to share with all of you what is right in front of you, ready to be your best friends and protectors and help you navigate through the pinball machine of life.

Acknowledgments

Special thanks to:

The New Dawn Foundation and sweat lodge communities. You provide me with a spiritual home and family.

Anne Dillon, Penney Leyshon, and Georges Leclere for all your wisdom and support.

The lived joyful experience of life with my children Tania, Tristan, Terence, and Talia. You've provided me with a wealth of information about growing up and love.

My spirit guides who not only helped me write this book but also are with me constantly providing support and love.

I am also tremendously grateful to my clients around the world. All the stories come from my clients. By helping you all, I have learned so much. This is our story, yours and mine, that will hopefully help so many more people.

Suggested Reading

Animal Speak: The Spiritual & Magical Powers of Creatures Great & Small and
  Nature-Speak: Signs, Omens and Messages in Nature, by Ted Andrews
Black Elk: The Sacred Ways of a Lakota, by Wallace Black Elk and William S.
  Lyon
Defy Gravity: Healing Beyond the Bounds of Reason, by Carolyn Myss
Destiny of Souls and *Journey of Souls*, by Michael Newton
Embraced by the Light, by Betty J. Eadie
The Four Agreements and *The Mastery of Love*, by Don Miguel Ruiz
A Gift of Healing in a Handbook, by Penney Leyshon and Kathleen Spellman
Hanta Yo: An American Saga, by Ruth Beebe Hill
Life on the Other Side and *Past Lives, Future Healing*, by Sylvia Browne and
  Lindsay Harrison
Love Poems from God: Twelve Sacred Voices from the East and West, by Daniel
  Ladinsky
Loving What Is, by Byron Katie
Medicine Woman, by Lynn V. Andrews
Meditation and Mantras, by Swami Vishnu Devananda
Peace, Love and Healing, by Bernie S. Siegel, M.D.
Proof of Heaven: A Neurosurgeon's Journey into the Afterlife, by Eben Alexander
Second Sight, by Judith Orloff, M.D.
Shapeshifting, by John Perkins
You Can Heal Your Life, by Louise L. Hay

Index

About the Author

ALEXANDRA LECLERE is a clairvoyant, clairaudient, and clairsentient energy healer who uses her connection with the spirit world to help others heal by identifying and removing their personal obstacles to bring power and joy to their lives.

Alexandra helps people get in touch with their internal gifts by introducing them to their spirit guides and empowering them to connect to spirits and the spirit world. She also helps people learn about energy and how to use it to facilitate healing as well as contact loved ones who have passed in order to bring closure and comfort.

She leads workshops and seminars on spirit communication throughout the United States and abroad. She also mentors individuals who want to develop their healing abilities. Alexandra offers private sessions in person or virtually. Through one-on-one sessions she helps clients get in touch with their personal healing energy and intuition.

Alexandra's abilities are enhanced by personal empathy formed through her own experiences of abuse. She has been able to open the door to her dark room and let in the light. Now it is her life's work to bring the light to others. She is tremendously grateful for her gifts and eager to share them with everyone.

Prior to finding her gifts of mediumship and healing, Alexandra was president of an international television production and multimedia corporation for seventeen years. She is currently president of the New Dawn Foundation in New Rochelle, New York, where she sees clients. Alexandra leads regular sweat lodge ceremonies there. She is also active in the Presbyterian Church.

Books of Related Interest

Seeing the Dead, Talking with Spirits
Shamanic Healing through Contact with the Spirit World
by Alexandra Leclere
Foreword by John Perkins

Spirit Speaker
A Medium's Guide to Death and Dying
by Salicrow

Angels in Waiting
How to Reach Out to Your Guardian Angels and Spirit Guides
by Robbie Holz with Judy Katz

The Persistence of the Soul
Mediums, Spirit Visitations, and Afterlife Communication
by Mark Ireland

An Energy Healer's Book of Dying
For Caregivers and Those in Transition
by Suzanne Worthley

Lessons from the Afterlife
A Deep Knowledge Meditation Guidebook
by Matthew McKay, Ph.D.

7 Reasons to Believe in the Afterlife
A Doctor Reviews the Case for Consciousness after Death
by Jean Jacques Charbonier, M.D.

Ancestral Medicine
Rituals for Personal and Family Healing
by Daniel Foor, Ph.D.

INNER TRADITIONS • BEAR & COMPANY
P.O. Box 388 • Rochester, VT 05767
1-800-246-8648 • www.InnerTraditions.com

Or contact your local bookseller